11/01

3000 800023 050
St. Louis Community College

D0944816

An Early Florida Adventure Story

The Florida Heritage Series

Florida A&M University, Tallahassee
Florida Atlantic University, Boca Raton
Florida Gulf Coast University, Fort Myers
Florida International University, Miami
Florida State University, Tallahassee
University of Central Florida, Orlando
University of Florida, Gainesville
University of North Florida, Jacksonville
University of South Florida, Tampa
University of West Florida, Pensacola

THE FLORIDA HERITAGE SERIES

*Indian Art of Ancient Florida*, by Barbara Purdy with photos by Roy C. Craven, Jr. (1996)

*A History of Florida through New World Maps: Borders of Paradise*,
edited by Dana M. Ste Claire (1997)

*An Atlas of Maritime Florida*, by Roger C. Smith, James J. Miller,
Sean M. Kelley, and Linda G. Harbin (1997)

*Florida's History through Its Places: Properties in the National Register of Historic Places*,
by Morton D. Winsberg (1997)

*Hernando de Soto among the Apalachee: The Archaeology of the First Winter Encampment*, by
Charles R. Ewen and John H. Hann (1998)

*The Apalachee Indians and Mission San Luis*,
by John H. Hann and Bonnie G. McEwan (1998)

*Florida's Indians from Ancient Times to the Present*, by Jerald T. Milanich (1998)

*Spanish Colonial Silver Coins in the Florida Collection*, by Alan K. Craig (2000)

*Spanish Colonial Gold Coins in the Florida Collection*, by Alan K. Craig (2000)

*An Early Florida Adventure Story*, by Fray Andrés De San Miguel,
translated by John H. Hann (2000)

# An Early Florida Adventure Story

❧❧❧

## by Fray Andrés de San Miguel
## Translated by John H. Hann

Foreword by James J. Miller

Florida Bureau of Archaeological Research
Division of Historical Resources

University Press of Florida
Gainesville · Tallahassee · Tampa · Boca Raton
Pensacola · Orlando · Miami · Jacksonville · Ft. Myers

A Florida Heritage Publication

06  05  04  03  02  01  6  5  4  3  2  1

Library of Congress Cataloging-in-Publication Data
Andrés de San Miguel, fray, 1577–1644?
An early Florida adventure story / by Fray Andrés de San Miguel; translated by
John H. Hann; foreword  by James J. Miller.
p. cm.
Translated from "Dos antiguas relaciones de la Florida" published by Genaro
García (1902)—Publisher's  note.
Includes bibliographical references and index.
ISBN 0-8130-1876-5 (alk. paper)
1. Andrés de San Miguel, fray, 1577–1644? 2. Florida—History—Spanish colony,
1565–1763. 3. Georgia—History—Colonial period, ca. 1600–1775. 4. Nuestra
Señora de la Merced (Ship). 5. Shipwrecks—Florida—History—16th century.
6. Indians of North America—Missions—Florida—History—16th century.
7. Indians of North America—Missions—Georgia—History—16th century.
8. Sailors—Spain—Biography. 9. Saint Augustine (Fla.)—History—16th century.
I. Hann, John H. II. Dos antiguas relaciones de la Florida. English. 2000. III. Title.
F314.A53  2000
975.9'01—dc21  00-061601

The University Press of Florida is the scholarly publishing agency for the State
University System of Florida, comprising Florida A & M University, Florida
Atlantic University, Florida Gulf Coast University, Florida International University,
Florida State University, University of Central Florida, University of Florida,
University of North Florida, University of South Florida, and University of
West Florida.

University Press of Florida
15 Northwest 15th Street
Gainesville, FL 32611-2079
http://www.upf.com

To my sisters,

Kathleen M. FitzGerald and Edna P. McNamara

# Contents

Acknowledgments ix

Foreword by James J. Miller xi

Part 1. Introduction by John H. Hann 1

Part 2. Fray Andrés de San Miguel:
An Introductory Essay by
Genero García 11

Part 3. Account Written by Fray Andrés de San Miguel 23

Translator's Notes by John H. Hann 97

Index 105

————

Map of Fray Andrés's landings 54

# Acknowledgments

Bonnie G. McEwan provided a valuable critique of an early draft of the translation and encouragement and support for my completion of the project. I am grateful also for the encouragement from Jim Miller, chief of the Florida Bureau of Archaeological Research. I thank Terri White for putting my typescript onto the computer and Elyse Cornelison for transforming that early computer copy into one that met the press's specifications and incorporated substantial editing. I am thankful to her also for her work on the map. I am grateful for the press's two readers' many helpful suggestions for improving the manuscript.

# Foreword

What lover of history has not been captivated by the fabulous narratives of Florida's exploration and discovery? Such accounts as William Bartram's *Travels*, Jonathan Dickinson's *Journal*, the *Relation* of Cabeza de Vaca, the four de Soto chronicles, Fontaneda's *Memoir*, and Jacques Le Moyne's *Narrative* with the de Bry engravings enrich and enliven the first centuries of Florida's European history. These are stories of wonder, of tragedy, of great human loss, of religious persecution, and the first human contact between profoundly different cultures. They are compelling not only because they tell something of life centuries ago but also because they reveal the human mind and spirit under the most trying conditions.

In *An Early Florida Adventure Story*, John Hann has translated and introduced a powerful late-sixteenth-century account centered in Florida and Georgia from a time when missions were just being established among the Guale Indians. The story of Fray Andrés de San Miguel began when he was in his late teens on a 1595 voyage from Havana to Spain aboard a vessel in the Spanish Plate Fleet. Andrés de Segura, as he was known before joining the Carmelite Order, had the fortune to serve on the *Nuestra Señora de la Merced*, a *nao* built in Seville. Following the usual delays for weather and bureaucracy, the fleet left Havana in March and followed the Gulf Stream north through the Straits of Florida along the east coast of the peninsula.

Above the latitude of Cape Canaveral a terrible storm arose, battering the fleet and the *Merced* for four days. At the next dawn it became clear that the *Merced* had been separated from the fleet and had nearly been demolished. The crew labored mightily for days, but water entered the shattered hull faster than it could be pumped out. When half the crew conspired to escape in the ship's only launch, Andrés and his companions were left to save themselves from a sinking ship. In a series of events which measure the worth of men, the remaining crew built a makeshift boat in the form of a box and abandoned the sinking vessel. Seven sailors remained with the ship, unsure of which death was more certain. Andrés and his companions spent another twelve days at sea with little food or water and with waning strength and hope.

Their "landing" in the Georgia Sea Islands near the mouth of the Altamaha River ensured their survival and brought them in contact with the Guale Indians of Talaje and Asao, then eventually to St. Augustine. Andrés's adventures included another contact with Native people, this time in South Florida. Finally, after 111 days, he returned to Havana. The narrative of his personal saga concludes with his eyewitness account of the English siege and burning of Cádiz in 1696.

These events undoubtedly had a lasting effect on the young man. Two years later Andrés de Segura returned to Mexico to join the Carmelite Order as a lay brother, keeping the vow he made to give his life to God should he survive the shipwreck. In Mexico City he practiced architecture and mathematics, designed and built many Carmelite structures, and served as hydrographic expert for the second stage of the drainage of the Valley of Mexico.

Works like these have a literary, a philosophical, and a historical life. They represent the telling of a dramatic tale, reflecting unusual literary conventions and styles that are all the more powerful for their age. Often, such accounts portray profound events involving matters of life and death and hardships that seem unreal to us today. Philosophically, they reveal a fundamental and unquestioned belief in Almighty God, whose providence is always gratefully acknowledged, however tragic the outcome. Finally, however flawed in objectivity or foreign in time or culture, these narratives are the primary documents of which history is made, the pieces from which we try to re-create what happened in the past. Their words and constructions are analogous to the artifacts and associations with which archaeologists try to re-create the past. These historical accounts are not "photographic" records of history but rather a complex product of personality, cultures, and events that are to be untangled. They constitute evidence rather than reality, and from them we construct our own modern version of the facts.

John Hann has brought this account to modern English-speaking readers for the first time. Although published in Spanish in 1902, the work was available only in a limited edition and has not been well known to researchers. Its many objective observations on the Native people of Florida and Georgia provide a rich account of architecture, customs, social and political organization, technology, environment, and behavior at the earliest stages of missionization. We can easily recognize many of the important elements of southeastern Indian society such as council houses, clothing styles, the black drink ceremony, and the chunkey game. Like a newly discovered manuscript of a famous author, Hann's *Early Florida Adventure Story* is now added to the short list of sixteenth-century Florida accounts that are at once important history and powerful literature.

James J. Miller,
State Archaeologist

# Part I

## Introduction

DURING THE HEYDAY OF Spain's establishment of its control over the major portion of the New World, numberless individuals' lives were influenced dramatically by their early experiences with the realities of this "wondrous New World." Unfortunately, far too few of those fortune seekers have left us any account of their most memorable experiences or reflections on what they observed and experienced in that tumultuous enterprise. A notable exception is a relatively brief account from the year 1595 penned by a young Spaniard shipwrecked off the Spanish Florida coast of what is now the state of Georgia. That experience drastically altered the course of his life. At the height of the storm when it appeared that he and all his shipmates were lost, he made a vow that, if he survived, he would devote his life to the service of God.

This teenage lad, who then bore the name of Andrés de Segura, is known to history as Fray Andrés de San Miguel, a Carmelite lay brother who was responsible for the design and building of many of the major establishments of his order in early seventeenth-century Mexico. A man of many talents, he also played an important role in the second stage of the drainage of the Valley of Mexico to rectify the errors of the first efforts linked to that enterprise. Modern inhabitants of Florida and Georgia can be grateful that he took the time to pen an account of the dramatic interludes of the shipwreck and his descriptions of the Indians he encountered along the coasts of Georgia and Florida. Historians and others will value the penetrating light his account throws on the spirit of the age as perceived by an idealistic youth, influenced undoubtedly by his adoption of a monastic vocation as a consequence of those early experiences.

Fray Andrés presents a cold-eyed look at what the experiences of sailing could be in the late sixteenth century. He describes how, while sailing, the official fleet's flagship rolled violently, throwing six of its crew or passengers into the sea. They were allowed to drown "because they did not wish to swing the vessel around" to wait for the "swimmers or to put out the launch to pick them out." He comments also on deficiencies in the sailing arrangements by which ships were chosen for Spain's silver-carrying fleets and armadas and on the costly hurried careening of ships that had sat idle for many months. After those ships had attracted most of the experienced officers, the rest of the shipowners, desiring to get to Spain in order to return with the following year's fleets, bought costly permissions to sail with the fleet. They then had insufficient time to prepare their ships adequately or to acquire experienced officers. He criticizes the fleet system sharply as well as the petty motives that guided those who were in charge that made it impossible for the fleet to sail on time. The result was an unplanned wintering over that added two million pesos to the fleets' expenditures. He concludes this critique, "Ordinarily, the disasters and losses that happen on the sea are of this sort, resulting from the greed or neglect of those who are in command."

His account gives us an introspective limning of the thought processes, concerns, ambitions, and religiosity of the age. Its apt reflection of the age's Catholicism is epitomized in his remark that "in the midst of such great carelessness, some remembrance of God was not lacking and a great deal [of remembrance] of the Virgin Most Pure, and in particular of the one of Mercy, because that was the name of the ship, by whose intercession we believed all of us received such great mercies from God, ones such as we have never heard of from a shipwreck."

Although his account appears to have been written some years after the event (based on internal evidence), it presents a remarkable reflection on the undaunted spirit of the young people among the crew and passengers, who were largely immune to the discouragement and depression of those in charge and of those who, in normal times, boasted most about their courage and bravery and enterprise. As the threat represented by the storm became apparent, all of the latter crawled into holes of their own to await what they regarded as inevitable death, except for the ship's valiant purser. It was he who organized and, where necessary, bullied the young men into manning the pumps to keep the ship afloat through the storm. When those who had been in charge and their clique, coming out of their holes when the storm ended, commandeered the ship's launch and took off with the ship's carpenter and tools, leaving the rest behind to go down with the ship, the purser oversaw the building of an unstable makeshift sloop on which those who remained, who had the courage to board it, eventually reached land.

Andrés de Segura set out for the New World from Spain in 1593 as a youth of about sixteen to seek his fortune on a newly built ship named *Our Lady of Mercy*. The fleet in which his ship sailed remained almost a year at Mexico's port of San Juan de Ulloa waiting for silver for its return voyage to Spain scheduled for the summer of 1594. On finally leaving Mexico in mid-July, the fleet's unduly long sixty-two-day sail to Havana to join the fleet bearing South America's silver required another stay there because of the approach of winter and its storms. Thus the fleets did not set sail for Spain until March 1595.

During the months Andrés was in Havana over the winter of 1594–95 he witnessed the aftermath of an important event in Florida that has received little attention in its standard histories. He records seeing some imprisoned men brought from Florida "in a flyboat because they had killed their governor." He notes that they were tried and executed while he was in Havana and their heads put on display throughout the city. Their leader, dispatched to Spain in the fleet in which Andrés sailed in March, perished in the storm that brought Andrés his shipwreck experience, along with another prisoner whom Andrés identifies only as a "Portuguese . . . arrested in Puebla de los Angeles because he very much resembled don Antonio."

The event in Florida to which he refers is a 1592 mutiny by soldiers at St. Augustine in which they deposed and imprisoned the unpopular governor, Gutierre de Miranda, while proclaiming continued loyalty to the king. The soldiers did not kill the governor outright, but he died in their hands before Havana's governor could arrange for sending Miranda to Cuba. Deposing the fort's commander as well, the soldiers elected a Captain Francisco de Salazar as their commander. As a stopgap to preserve the appearance of legitimacy, Havana's governor named Salazar acting governor, but suggested he be replaced as soon as possible.

The soldiers' grievance was largely monetary. Reportedly, they had received none of their cash salary for five years prior to the revolt. Andrés records hearsay that when the governor's agent collected the money in Mexico, Miranda transformed much of the soldier's pay into clothing, forcing them to accept the clothing as payment "with very swollen profits" for himself. What seems to have driven the soldiers to mutiny was news of the death of Rodrigo de Junco—a new governor whom the king had sent to succeed Miranda—when the ship Junco had boarded in Havana sank with all aboard on its way to St. Augustine.[1] Although Spain quickly learned about this contretemps, a series of circumstances slowed the authorities' effective response. One early prospect turned the post down flatly. Pedro Menéndez Marqués, a logical choice in view of his experience and prestige in Florida, was not anxious to return and fended off the initial offers. Although he assented when the Crown finally met his financial demands and although he had assembled forces and supplies on the readied fleet, he developed a severe illness just as the fleet was ready to leave, forcing the Crown to turn to Domingo Martínez de Avendaño, who had been seriously considered for the post earlier.[2]

The "don Antonio" whom Andrés mentions on that occasion was, undoubtedly, the pretender to the Portuguese throne known as Antonio, Prior of Crato. The pretender Antonio was an illegitimate son of Luis, a son of Portugal's King Manuel I (1495–1521). When Philip II of Spain forcefully asserted his claim to Portugal's throne in 1580, "the prior of Crato was the only candidate," as A. H. Oliveira Marques phrased it, "brave enough to defy the might of Philip II."[3]

The experiences that Andrés recounts in this narrative occurred in 1595 while he was returning to Spain on the same vessel. Five days out of Havana, as the fleet was coming out of the Bahama Channel, a storm arose that damaged *Our Lady of Mercy* badly and left it leaking dangerously. The small clique who seized the ship's launch not long after the storm ended abandoned the thirty-seven who were left on board, expecting that they would go down with the ship. Those left on board cajoled a depressed and mentally unstable caulker into attempting to build a vessel Andrés describes as "a long box, tall and narrow," using not very suitable pieces of lumber pulled from the ship's superstructure. Thirty people, who represented its capacity, reached land with it on an island that probably was Wolf Island or Little St. Simons Island at the mouth of the Altamaha River. The other seven chose not to entrust their lives to such a makeshift vessel.

These survivors established contact eventually with Guale Indians from the village of Asao located on the lower Altamaha. The Guale proved to be friendly, although the permanent mission among them had not yet been established. Assisted by the Indians, the shipwrecked Spaniards made their way southward to the San Pedro Mocama mission among the Timucua-speaking Mocama on Cumberland Island, then the northernmost of the missions. The Mocama's Fray Baltasar López was absent at the time, probably on one of his many missionary forays to Timucua-speaking villages on the adjacent mainland. Andrés's remark that San Pedro was without a friar at that time is borne out by an order from the king to Florida's governor on June 18, 1595, instructing him to return the friar to San Pedro's Cacique Don Juan as one who had always been a friend of the Spaniards and had given them supplies worth over 9,000 reales.[4] Governor Martínez de Avendaño, while still in Havana, noted that Acting Governor Salazar had given permission for a number of Florida's Franciscans to leave the province. He observed that the departure had not been voluntary in the case of Fray Juan Mesquita and that it represented a serious loss, as he had been in Florida a long time and was a "tongue" or interpreter.[5]

After the survivors had spent about two weeks there, a Spanish vessel carried them on to St. Augustine. Andrés's account of his experiences among the Indians of the Georgia coast is particularly rich in ethnographic details related to their structures, food, clothing, games, government, and the like.

Andrés and most of his comrades were fortunate that the garrison at St. Augustine was not shorthanded when they reached that port. He stated that the majority of its soldiers had reached there as shipwreck survivors and had been forced to remain there in military service. Only a couple of Flemish artillerymen from his group were pressed into service at St. Augustine, along with one other young man, a gunsmith, who was kept because the existing one was old. The governor ordered that the shipwreck survivors be given a daily ration at the king's expense—as though they were soldiers during their month-long stay—as well as a special allowance of twenty-five pounds of flour and a good quantity of jerky for the trip to Havana.

The vessel that carried them to Havana sailed close to shore from point to point, providing them with many trading encounters with the Indians on the coast and, farther south, an opportunity to observe the natives' technique for killing whales in the inshore waters. That leg of Andrés's voyage did not lack for adventure either. In south Florida waters, two English vessels captured their small boat. After stripping them of their more valuable property, the Englishmen released them to go on to Havana, which they reached 111 days after having sailed from there on *Our Lady of Mercy* on March 11, 1595, headed for Spain.

Andrés returned to Cádiz in 1596 just in time to witness the British attack on and capture, pillaging, and destruction of that Spanish port city. He had set out for the New World from there in 1593. His account ends with his report on that episode of Spanish history, emphasizing again an abdication of leadership by those in charge of the city's defense that facilitated the success of the invaders.

Having made a promise to give his life to God should he survive the foundering of his ship, Fray Andrés returned to Mexico in 1598 to join the Carmelite Order as a simple lay brother. Prior to that, he had received some training in mathematics during a stay in Seville. In Mexico, he specialized in architecture and mathematics, studying hydrography as well.

Fray Andrés's account contains a few historical inaccuracies based on information that he garnered from his conversations with the soldiers during his stay in St. Augustine, his faulty recollection of them, or in other cases (pertaining to the Franciscans) the inadequacy of his sources. He places the beginning of the Franciscans' work in Florida in 1595 rather than 1573, when the first Franciscans arrived to take up the work the Jesuits had abandoned. He places the newly founded Asao mission of 1595 erroneously on St. Simons Island. It did move to the island sometime later, but was still on the Altamaha River at least as late as 1604.

Fray Andrés seems to have been led into this error in part by an overweening belief that God had been using him and his comrades throughout this disaster to prepare the way for the Florida missions. In concluding remarks about their experiences among the Guale, he states:

I will say lastly that it seems God had [a hand] in bringing us to them. For these two chiefs [of Asao and Talaje] are now embarking and going with us and they were baptized in St. Augustine. . . . After they were baptized they asked for ministers in their land. . . . And because there was no more than one very old cleric in all of Florida, the governor sent to Havana to ask for religious and [some] from the order of St. Francis came on the same frigate that brought us to Havana. This was the beginning and origin that this sacred order had in Florida. Who would think that with troubles, losses, and paths [that are] twisting and wandering from our point of view, that

God was directing them toward such lofty goals as the conversion of many of these poor souls to whom nobody had paid any attention because they had neither gold nor silver. And God determined our path in such a way that in all the districts where we were, both populated and unpopulated, the first five convents were established. . . . And thus God has gathered more fruit from these kingdoms by means of our troubles and losses than from all the expeditions the Spaniards have made in them.

His other errors are more straightforward. Most prominent among them is the confusion by Andrés or his soldier informants of Pedro Menéndez Marquéz with his uncle, Pedro Menéndez de Avilés. In telling of events that occurred in the 1560s in which Pedro Menéndez de Avilés was the major protagonist, Fray Andrés's account makes Pedro Menéndez Marquéz the sole protagonist. Such errors of fact will be pointed out and corrected in notes to the translation text.

The Mexican bibliophile Genaro García brought this manuscript to light almost a century ago in a volume he published in 1902 in Spanish under the title *Dos Antiguas Relaciones de la Florida* (Two ancient accounts about Florida). The first of those "two ancient reports" in García's book was Bartolomé Barrientos's "Los Naturales de America bajo la Dominación Española" (The natives of America under Spanish domination), which the University of Florida Press published in 1965 in a translation by Anthony Kerrigan under the title *Pedro Menéndez de Avilés, Founder of Florida*. The second part was Fray Andrés's report, which is presented here in translation.

The original manuscript of Fray Andrés's *Relacion* recounting his adventures of 1595–96 is presently part of the Genaro García Collection housed in the University of Texas Latin American Collection Library. The manuscript appears toward the end of a bound volume sandwiched between two treatises by Fray Andrés on hydrography. Its location in that volume suggests that the manuscript, in its present form at least, was written relatively late in Fray Andrés's career—during the time that he was involved in the second stage of the drainage of the Valley of Mexico, where Hernán Cortés built his beginning stage of Mexico City as successor to the Aztec's Tenochtitlan, an island-city in the middle of a lake. (The translator is grateful to the University of Texas Library for making a microfilm copy of Fray Andrés's manuscripts available to him.)

García devoted the first chapter of his 1902 volume to Bio-Bibliographic Reports about Bartolomé Barrientos and Fray Andrés de San Miguel. The portion of that chapter that pertains to Fray Andrés will be presented here in translation.

## Translator's Note

Occasionally I have placed a question mark after a word. In no instance do such question marks indicate that Andrés's writing was indecipherable or difficult to decipher. Instead they are meant to indicate uncertainty, for various reasons, over the propriety of my rendition of a certain word or phrase. In some instances, as in my translation of *arregoces* as Aragonese, it indicates that I had some doubts about the correctness of that translation inasmuch as *arregoces* does not appear in modern Spanish. In other cases, as in my rendition of *guarneserla* as "to prime it," I am indicating that dictionaries do not give "to prime" as a meaning of *guarnecer*. In still other instances, as with *quejeron*, which I rendered as "they wished," the question mark signifies that Andrés's spelling of the word is sufficiently different from the one used today as to leave some uncertainty about the propriety of that rendition. In a few cases, the question mark indicates that the Spanish word has other meanings that also fit the context, highlighting the reality that translating involves a certain amount of interpretation.

That reality gave rise to the Portuguese saying that "to translate is to betray." That danger is reflected as well in the English word *traduce*, the cognate of the Spanish *traducir* meaning "to translate."

## Notes

1. Juan de Texeda to king, Havana, March 22, May 5, 1593. Archivo General de Indias, Santo Domingo (hereafter AGI, SD) 99, Stetson Collection (hereafter SC); Pedro Menéndez Marqués to king, Seville, June 5, July 30, 1593, AGI, Indiferente General (hereafter IG) 1103.

2. Council of the Indies, Madrid, February 1, 1594, AGI, SD 6, SC; Pedro Menéndez Marqués to king, Seville, July 30, September 10, 1593, AGI, IG 1103, SC.

3. A. H. de Oliveira Marques, *History of Portugal,* 2d ed. (New York: Columbia University Press, 1976), 312–14.

4. Royal decree, Madrid, June 18, 1595, to Domingo Martínez de Avendaño, AGI, SD 2528, SC.

5. Domingo Martínez de Avendaño to king, Havana, May 9, 1594, AGI, SD 125, SC.

# Part 2

Fray Andrés de San Miguel
"Account of the Difficulties That the People of a
Ship Called *The Lady of Mercy* Endured and About
Some Things That Occurred in That Fleet" [Relación
de los Trabajos Que la Gente de Vna Nao Llamada
Nra Señora de la Merced Padeció y de Algunas Cosas
Que en Aquella Flota Sucedieron]

Genaro García's prefatory remarks about
Fray Andrés de San Miguel (pp. xviii–xxvii)

Translated by John H. Hann

WE READ IN AN important unpublished work of the mid-seventeenth century that this illustrious man was born in Medina Sidonia in the year of 1577;[1] he was named Andrés de Segura. His parents, "although well born, were poor; they had other sons, and in this one Heaven had deposited much courage, a generous spirit, and so capable and profound an understanding that, if destiny had steered him into the Schools, he would have been a wonder of many centuries. He combined with this a frankness and sincerity and more inclination toward the honorable than the common propensity of our corrupted clay is wont to make manifest in [one] of so tender years."[2]

Andrés was only fifteen years old around 1592 when, in search of fortune and following the example of so many of his compatriots, he resolved to cross over to this New World, which he did not succeed in doing until the following year, weighing anchor from Cádiz on board a resplendent and gallant vessel (*nao*) named *Our Lady of Mercy*.

Our Andrés accurately describes this voyage in a very detailed manner in the *Relación* which we publish for the first time today.

Fray Manuel de San Gerónimo writes that the shipwreck of the *nao* opposite the east coast of Florida having become imminent, Andrés "made a vow to become a religious of the Order of Mary Most Holy of Carmen, if Her Majesty should bring him out alive from this danger."[3]

Andrés, having returned to Spain at the end of 1595, poorer than when he left her, but already a profound understander of men, of whose brutal selfishness he had full and abundant proofs, hastened to return to the Indies to fulfill his religious vow there.

Thus he set sail for the second time in 1597 headed for New Spain; having arrived there, in the following year he took the habit as a lay brother in the Convent of the Carmen of Puebla [Carmelites]. His exceptional gifts would have permitted him to achieve easily the most honored posts of the order; however, he did not wish to aspire to them, and, instead, with refined modesty he determined to remain a lay brother until his death, "a decision from which they could not turn him aside, even though the Religious tried to, on seeing his great capacity and aptitude for any employment whatsoever."[4]

From then on Fray Andrés devoted himself to the exercise of the virtue to which his essentially kindly soul called him, and at the same time he dedicated himself to cultivating the sciences with that very capacious and deep understanding of his. For this, he was seen frequently to shut himself up in his cell.

This exceptional application to study, combined with his vast natural intelligence and his natural spirit of exact observation, soon made him excel in mathematics, geography, astronomy, hydrography, and architecture, which "he succeeded in understanding like the best of his century."[5] "It is difficult to say (Fray Marcial de San Juan Bautista explains) how much honor and splendor he brought to his order both with the abundance of his virtues and with the excellence of his genius and his very deep knowledge in mathematics."[6]

Once Fray Andrés was instructed sufficiently, he began to utilize his knowledge and talent for the benefit of his order and of the public. It was he who constructed the convents of Celaya, of Desierto, and of Queretaro, and the Colegio of San Angel. At the request of the Viceroy Marquis de Cerralvo, it was he also who designed the works that were to alleviate the problems produced in Mexico City by the inundation of 1629 [resulting from deficiencies of the first attempt at draining the valley of Mexico]. It was he who, finally, various years later under Viceroy Marquis de Cadereita, undertook the draining of the valley, securing the opening of a ditch forty *estados* [2.17 yards] deep, which is still being used today, and, in its width, with a capacity for two wagons (*galeras*), "in contrast to what had been done up to then by Enrico Martínez with an excessive expenditure of money and at the cost of the death of many Indians."[7] Fray Manuel de San Juan Crisóstomo had reason thus for saying that our beautiful city owes its existence to Fray Andrés.[8] Fray Pablo Antonio del Niño Jesús repeated the same thing.[9]

Fray Andrés himself explains: "With the city of Mexico being in the miserable state in which we have seen it in the year of 29, he [fray Andrés] gave a report to the Señor Marquis de Cerralvo in which he said that, if the river of Quautitlan were to rise with the new cut (*sanja*), with the weight and force of the water that would enter by way of this in the outflow (*desagüe*), it would be possible to open at a cut the entire tunnel (*socabon*) (projected by Enrico Martínez and blocked at the time by sinking (*hundimiento*) of the land), as a result of which it appeared that it would be possible to repair the damage to the city. But as it appeared to him that it required (*pedia*) many people, he did not accept it. Later he gave him another report for the same by way of a shorter path in the drainage (*desagüe*). But, as he once again came to agree with Henrico Martínez, nothing came of it."[10]

His prestige grew so much that, as we have indicated already, in the words of Beristáin y Sousa, Fray Andrés managed to become "the universal consultant for the entire kingdom in the fields of architecture, mechanics, and hidraulics."[11]

"Finally, when he was already full of years and aches, obedience brought him to the directing of the building of this convent of Guazindeo or Salvatierra. He drew up the plans, gave shape to the manner of doing it, and for some time he presided over the work, as far as he was able to, to the great edification of everyone."[12] While he was so engaged, death surprised him around 1644.

Although numerous, the treatises and reports by Fray Andrés remained almost totally unknown to historians and bibliographers. Fray Manuel de San Gerónimo[13] speaks of only five treatises. Fray Marcial de San Juan Bautista[14] and Fray Cosme de Villiers de San Esteban[15] list as many more. Don Juan José de Eguiaren y Eguren reduced the said treatises to four[16] and don Andrés González Barcia[17] to three. Beristáin y Sousa could have given us a sufficiently complete catalog of the works of Fray Andrés because of having had almost all of them in his hands, but he contented himself, notwithstanding, with enumerating only eight.[18]

It fell to our acknowledged bibliophile Don José María de Agreda y Sánchez to publish the said catalog[19] for the first time, consisting of twenty-five titles to which we are adding for our part the two reports written in 1629, about which Fray Andrés himself spoke to us.[20]

From all his works, the report (*informe*) of 1636 is the only one that has been printed up to now. Perhaps we will be able to publish its counterpart (*complemento*), which is the Account (*Relación*) of the site, works, and state of the city of Mexico and about the remedy for it.

Fray Marcial de San Juan Bautista wrote in 1730 that the writings of our author were preserved in the convent of Puebla (Angelopolitanum) of the Carmelite religious,[21] and González Barcia,[22] Villiers de San Esteban,[23] and Eguiara y Eguren [sic][24] repeated the same thing. Beristáin y Souza contradicts them in a certain manner, considering that he gives assurances about having seen the writings alluded to in the library of the Colegio de San Angel.[25]

The señor de Agreda y Sánchez is of the opinion: "that they were never in the convent of Puebla de los Angeles and that father Fray Marcial, not having exact reports about the convents and colleges belonging to the province of St. Albert (of New Spain) because he was not Spanish but French rather and. . . . never came here, made a mistake because of the resemblance between the names, both of which involved 'angel.' For the name Angelopolitano was applied to the said convent of Puebla because of the name of that city in which it was founded and to the College because of the saint who was their titular during many years, so it was said to be of San Angelo. And it has been so named even after that saint no longer served as its titular."[26] Be that as it may, it is known to many that as a consequence of the Liberals' decree issued in 1859, the Carmelites who dwelt in the Colegio de San Angel were secularized [and expelled]. And as a result of this the works of Fray Andrés passed into the possession of the recognized and esteemed bibliophile Don José María Andrade, from whom his nephew inherited them, my generous friend, the very learned and tireless bibliographer, señor canon don Vicente de P. Andrade.

Let us now get down to discussing the *Relación* that is published in this book.

Not because Fray Andrés wrote almost half a century later than Barrientos was he more fortunate in errors of spelling. Accordingly, except for some slight differences such as the undue suppression of one or more letters, which that one makes in various words, what we have said about this matter in the preceding chapter [dedicated to comments on the Barrientos manuscript] should be applied also, making allowance for the differences, to the text of the *Relación*.

Independently of the unquestionable merit that this one exhibits, there is the factor of its having been written by a witness of the events that are included in it, other circumstances exist that make it doubly valuable, such as its constant truth, its delicate beauty, its natural grace and of exquisite taste, the ingenuous faithfulness of the characters, the dramatic interest sustained without effort, and the fruitful teachings in which it abounds.

Petty human motives did not affect Fray Andrés; nor did the passions that blind one. Undisturbed, he weighed and assayed with serene tranquility and, on one single scale his own actions and those of others without regard for any influence whatever other than that pertaining to eternal truth. From this perspective (*arte*) we hear him praise the natives as docile, generous, and obliging and accuse the Castilians as ambitious, not very diligent in spreading the Christian faith, and, above all, inhumanely cruel, falling suddenly during the night on such and such native villages "and the soldiery spread all through it. And each one at the same time set fire to his part and kept guard over the doors of the houses that were burning, so that those who were inside should not come out. And on understanding that many Indians were coming together, they withdrew to their vessels, where they defended themselves with the harquebuses and returned to their presidio, leaving behind many deaths. And with these assaults, they kept everyone fearful, checked, and oppressed."[27]

Equally as [he writes] with truth, Fray Andrés writes with perfect beauty: the unexpected appearance of the little native boys with bows and arrows proportioned to their bodies, who set themselves to shooting toward the top of a tree "giggling joyfully."[28] It is an enchanting scene. The same can be said about the anxious arrival of the shipwreck victims on the island of Reynoso, described thus: "we set about approaching the land, and we saw that, with its being an open coast and without any shelter from all the ocean, the beach was of clean sand and the sea so gentle on it as if it were a small and sheltered pond. And so that we should recognize more clearly to whom we owed thanks and that it was God and not the launch that had brought us there, with the beach being so clean that there was no grain of sand to be found on it as big as a grain of wheat, and the sea, which was coming in, and so much without waves like a bowl of milk, when the launch began to touch the soft sand with its prow and so softly that it was scarcely felt, all of a sudden it fell over to one side as if it were tired of having kept itself upright for such a long time against its natural inclination."[29]

In other places Fray Andrés displays a most enjoyable grace, free of affectation; for example, when he speaks of the cat that, with a line (*rebenque*) around his throat awoke all the people of a vessel creating a tremendous alarm, and to which an old sailor who believed "it was a thing from the other life, said to it, on the part of God I command you to tell me who [you are] and what you wish."[30] Or when he refers to the imminent danger in which a Fleming was of being thrown into the sea who, because of the strength of his hunger and thirst "was not able to find a place to sit anywhere in the launch, with the result that he kept it unstable and put it in danger. And even though the purser and the rest reproached him, he did not quiet down, that he should not be able to continue (? *que no deuia de poder mas*)."[31]

As to what he does to the character of his protagonists, Fray Andrés succeeds in tracing them in a finished manner with few lines; the purser, among others, ready and energetic in action, who, when the vessel was on the point of capsizing, knew how to take charge of the demoralized crowd, to keep it under severe discipline at once, and, in the end, to save it. However, once he had fallen in love with the position of being in command, he did not want to relinquish it later and asked that he be honored with the name of captain and was usurping prerogatives that he had no claim to by right. This character trait (*personaje*) is the human type of many caudillos displayed in terrible moments of emergency, which our grandfathers have seen and which our grandsons also will see.

The author has an expert touch for instilling his scenes with deep dramatic interest. It throbs thus most vividly in the struggle that the thieving felons sustain in [the taking] of the sole launch that there was on the vessel that was about to sink and the unfortunate ones that followed it in an anguished swim because, with it, they lost their last hope of life. No less striking is the leaving behind of the cleric and the pilot: as "because of their tired old age and extreme weakness, they were not able to take a step, nor was there any strength among us for carrying them. The two of them agreed to remain there to die together consoling one another. And so that it might serve them as a shroud, because there was no hope of health, nor of sustenance, we brought them the sail from the launch in which we wrapped them. And leaving them thus with their heads uncovered and without them showing much grief nor sadness, we left them and made a start on our path."[32]

Out of the multiple lessons that may be drawn from the *Relación*, we point out two very close ones, to wit: that if this abandonment of the two old invalids reveals to us that man by a fatal law does not love his neighbor as [he does] himself, the earlier struggle reveals something more serious, the stolid selfishness that fills the depth of the human soul.

In summation: the *Relación* of Fray Andrés constitutes a precious jewel of the ancient historical literature in which there glows, deliciously mixed, the most exact truthfulness, the perennial sympathy for one's neighbor, simply because he is such, and the serene wisdom (*juicio*) that hits the mark in looking at everything in an unmistakable way, united with a strict moral standard (*moral justiciera*) that energetically condemns whatever is evil without prejudice or partialities and enthusiastically extols what is good.

## Notes [by Genaro García]

1. "Tesoro Escondido en el Monte Carmelo Mexicano" (Hidden Treasure in the Mexican Mount Carmel). Rich mine of examples and virtues; in the history of the discalced Carmelites of the province of New Spain. Discovered when written by Fray Augustín de la Madre de Dios, a religious of the same order. Book IV, Chapter 31. This work forms a tome in 4° of six preliminary sheets and 811 pages of text. It is divided into 5 books and each one of these into various chapters, some in blank, as is the 7th one of book V; others without having been finished, like the 32nd one of book IV, a chapter that happens to be precisely the second one among those destined for our Andrés. In general, it is a respectable work, worthy of seeing the public light because it encloses a great number of rare informations (*curiosas noticias*) that cannot be found in any other book. However it does not merit the exaggerated praise that Fray Anastasio de Santa Teresa showers on it, who did not hesitate to write: "our province of New Spain will be more famous because of the pen of father Fray Agustín as [well as] for his own achievements; more because of having written them with such great accuracy than for having accomplished them with universal admiration and benefit." (Page 366 of tome VII of the work cited in the following note.) We consider it as certain that the good Fray Anastasio took too seriously the remark made by Fray Agustín in the Note to the Reader that he had written his "Tesoro Escondido" under dictation from an angel. "And you should not be surprised," he adds seriously "that what I am saying to you was done by an angel."

2. Fray Manuel de San Gerónimo, in "Reforma de los Descalzos en Nvestra Señora del Carmen de la primitiva observancia . . ." (Reform of the discalced in Our Lady of Carmen of the primitive observance) by the priest Fray Francisco de Santa María (later by Fray José de Santa Teresa, Fray Manuel de San Gerónimo, and Fray Anastasio de Santa Teresa). In Madrid, by Diego Díaz de la Carrera (and others), 1644–1739. Tome VI, p. 254.

3. Work and tome cited, p. 256.

4. Fray Manuel de San Gerónimo, work and tome cited, p. 257.

5. *Ibidem*, p. 258.

6. *Bibliotheca Scriptorum utriusque Congregationes et Sexus Carmelitarum Excalceatorum* (Library of writers of both congregations and sexes of the Discalced Carmelites) (Burdigalae: Ex Tipographia Petri Sejourné, 1730), p. 17.

7. José María de Agreda y Sánchez, in *Anales del Museo Nacional de México* (Annals of the National Museum of Mexico) (México: Imprenta de Ignacio Escalante, 1877–1902), Tome IV, p. 169.

8. [In a] sermon that he preached during the festivity of the patronage of the Señor San José on the 24th of April of 1831 in the church of the Colegio de San Angel. (Méjico: Imprenta de Galvan, 1836), p. 31.

9. [In a] sermon that he preached on the 18th day of October of 1857 in the solemn function of the inauguration (*estreno*) of the church of the Colegio of the Carmelites of San Angel. (México: Imprenta de Ignacio Cumplido, 1857), p. 18.

10. *Anales del Museo Nacional de México,* Tome IV, p. 177.

11. *Op. cit.,* Tome II, p. 302.

12. Fray Manuel de San Gerónimo, work and tome cited, p. 259.

13. *Ibidem,* p. 260.

14. Work and page cited.

15. *Bibliotheca Carmelitana* (Carmelite library), notis criticis et dissertationibus illustrata: Aurelianis, Excudebant M. Couret de Villeneuve & Joannes Rouzeau Montaut, 1752, Tome I, col. 91.

16. *Op. cit.,* p. 128.

17. *Epitome,* Tome II, fols. MCCXII and MCCXXXVI front.

18. Work and page cited.

19. To wit:

1. Description of the temple of Solomon.

2. About some temples that there were in Peru and about their riches and ornateness.

3. How our temples are to be in imitation of the life of Jesuschrist, with some authorities and examples that the saints have left for us.

4. What sort of a thing is architecture. — About the foundations of the buildings. — About the thickness that the walls should have.

5. About mathematics. It is a treatise of geometry and trigonometry and it has many illustrations inserted.

6. About the building of the horizontal clocks and about that of the vertical ones traced with only a ruler and compass. It also has illustrations (*figuras*).

7. About Arithmetic.

8. About the measures that geometricians and cosmographers use.

9. About some reasons why a line cannot touch a circle in more than one point.

10. About some natural causes and reasons that there are for believing that the heavens (*cielos*) are just as firm as the earth is and the saints and learned men who affirm it.

11. About some of the reasonings on which the astronomers base the movement in the heavens and not in the stars and why the heavens are eleven, neither more nor less.

12. About the sphere of the sun and about its orbits (*orbes*). — About the orbits or circles of the other planets. — About the confused grandeur of the wheel (*rueda*) of the sun.

13. About some reasons that they state of Noah's ark having been measured with the common cubit (*codo comun*) and not with the geometric one. In this writing the author impugns the opinion that the Belgian medical man, Juan Goropio, registered (*estampó*) about this subject in his work entitled "*Origines Antuerpianae*" (Antwerp origins).

14. About how with ease one establishes how many grains of cabbage seed make a pile (*montón*) as big as the entire sphere of the world, land and water (*toda la esfera del mundo, tierra y agua*).

15. About the natural site and center of the waters and about how the sources (*manantiales*) of the springs (*fuentes*) and rivers have gone on in growth and for this reason all the seas. — About the natural origin and beginning of the springs and rivers. — About the natural cause why the springs and rivers have always been on the increase.

16. About Perspective. It has illustrations.

17. About architecture. One might say that this is the practical part. It has many drawings (*figuras*) of staircases, columns, doors, arches, carved and paneled ceilings (*artesonados*), altars, belfries (*campaniles*), vaults (*bovedas*), plans for buildings, etc.

18. Report (*Informe*) given to the Viceroy Marquis of Cadereita in the year of 1636 about the state of the works for the drainage of [the valley] of Mexico and about what it was appropriate to do. It is the one that now is being published. (In the same tome cited below, pp. 172–93.)

19. Account of the difficulties that the people of a ship called *Nuestra Señora de la Merced* endured, and about some things that occurred in that fleet. I believe that it would be appropriate to publish it also, as it contains a great variety of very rare reports (*noticias muy curiosas*), some of which interest us.

20. Hydraulics. It treats of the nature and location (*sitio*) of the waters, of the differences of the waters, of the signs (*indicios*) for finding hidden water, of the method of doing the draining (*de dar las sangrias*) of the flowing wells (*pozos manantiales*), about which waters may be most salubrious, about the hot waters, about the method for draining the mines, about the level, the method for making the sheets (*planchas*) or plates (*hojas*) of lead for the water pipes, the method for making the pipes of clay and of repairing them when they become broken. It has many drawings of aqueducts, pumps of various classes, siphon, levels, and tubes of piping.

21. About how one is to cover the roof (*tejado*) with sheets of lead and the method of making these for this object.

22. About how the glass windows (*vidrieras*) are made for the temples. It has two drawings.

23. Account of the location (*sitio*), works (*trabajos*), and state of the city of Mexico, and of the remedy for it, done for our Father General Fr. Esteban de San Josef, so that if it appears appropriate to his Reverence, he may place it in the hands of his Majesty. Year 1631. It has two drawings. This account is of importance. Because of this I believe that it should be published.

24. A brief treatise about the plants that have been grown best in this garden

of San Angelo.—About the peach-trees (*duraznos*), *priscos* (another variety of peach) and *melocotones* (a variety of peach).

25. Fray Andrés de San Miguel also wrote, and it appears to have been the last one that issued from his pen, a "Treatise about the degrees of grace that Mary Most Holy merited in the first one hundred acts of love of God that she made in her life." The chronicler general of the order mentioned him with these words.—In *Anales del Museo Nacional de México,* Tome IV, pp. 170–71.

20. He explains this, in addition: "About how it is possible for the work of the drainage to proceed up to the point of not leaving a trace of the lake in the one of Mexico, constantly cleaning all the land with the water, and the reasons why it is appropriate for the perpetuity of the drainage, not to leave a trace of the lake, he has given. . . . (sic) (to the Viceroy Marquis of Cadereita) *ample account* (*bastante relación*)."—*Ibidem,* p. 193. We do not know whether it was oral or written.

21. Work and page cited.

22. *Epitome,* tome and folios cited.

23. Work and tome cited, column 92.

24. Work and page cited.

25. Work and page cited.

26. *Op. cit.,* p. 171.

27. *Infra,* pp. 204–205.

28. *Infra,* p. 193.

29. *Infra,* p. 184.

30. *Infra,* p. 158.

31. *Infra,* p. 181.

32. *Infra,* p. 185.

# Part 3

## RELACION DE LOS TRABAJOS QUE LA GENTE DE VNA NAO LLA-MADA NRA SEÑORA DE LA MERCED PADECIO Y DE ALGUNAS COSAS QUE EN AQUE-LLA FLOTA SUCEDIE-RON

## Account of the Difficulties That the People of a Ship Called *The Lady of Mercy* En-dured and About Some Things That Oc-curred in That Fleet

Written by Fray Andrés de San Miguel
Translated by John H. Hann

THERE WAS A sword-maker in Seville successful in building a fortune. And so that his name might shine more and be better known, he became the owner of a ship (*nao*). And not wishing to purchase it, he built it among the smokestacks of Seville. He made it of great size and the ship emerged very gallant. Because of its being so, they selected it as flagship for the fleet that was going to New Spain in the year of ninety-two. As a consequence, the sword-maker, who had money, decorated it for the fiestas with the best and most costly pennants that must ever have been seen on the sea. They were of damask, with very good images of our Redeemer and of the most holy virgin and of saints. It had a flag and pennant for all the yard-arms and topmasts, quarterdecks and poop, and the areas covered with bunting. The pennants were so long that it was necessary to tie them up closely when there was no wind because a large part of them were wont to extend down to the sea.

This fleet of the year ninety-two was very unlucky in getting out over the bar of San Lucar because, on being readied three or four times for departure on various favorable tides, the wind was always contrary and it had to get ready once more. And when it did get out, winter had set in already. And as the memory was still so fresh of the fleet that had been lost in October of the year ninety off the coast of New Spain, they did not chance a departure that year. It remained to pass the winter imprisoned (*carcada*) in the bay of Cádiz where, when the fleet was entering, a large vessel belonging to Nicolás de Roda was burning. It was a new one on its first voyage. A son of his burned it while heating a kettleful of tar.

This fleet departed from Cádiz on the ninth of May of the following year of 1593 with more than sixty sails. It spent three days tacking about between Africa and Spain waiting for the completion of the loading of two galleons belonging to the *adelantado* [frontier governor] don Martín de Padilla so that they might accompany the fleet. One of these days two new vessels came into view and of some size. One of them came out for the rendevous missing a piece of its wales and the other one with a board crushed and shattered. Those of the wales saw the damage and soon remedied it. But those of the board either were not able or did not want to repair it. And on the eighth day after having sailed out of the bay, they abandoned it two musket shots distant from the island of la Palma without saving anything from it other than the people. Guile was said to have been involved because they had it insured and were thinking of collecting for it. But the vessel was lost and they did not cover it. This resulted from the waiting for the galleons. The fleet reached Ocaa on the eve of St. Johns without any other trouble having occurred than the vessel having burned in the bay and the one lost off La Palma. On the eighth day, after having taken on meat and water, and firewood, it set out for New Spain, where it was warmly awaited. And it was well received because they were still not drinking cocoa in that era and there were many natives. With the loss of the fleet of the year ninety and with this one's not having arrived in ninety-two, the land was very short of many things from Castile and of wine. So great was [the shortage] that it was issued by written orders like *pan de pocito* at a peso per pint. But once the fleet arrived, it soon returned to two reales and the rest of the things to their ordinary price. And in San Juan de Ulua a bottle of wine was worth four pesos and a cask a hundred. In this one can see the difference from those times, if they are compared with these. The two galleons were not able to enter into the port until it was readied, after many days. This was said about the one and it was the smaller one and it was called *The Crucifix*, that it carried two thousand kegs (*pipos*).[1]

The flagship and vessel belonging to the swordsmith made this entire voyage very gallantly. It was so swift sailing that it served as an advice-boat (*patacho*)[2] when necessary. But fond of the galleon *San Martín,* which was the largest among those of the *adelantado,* which was very swift sailing and of a beautiful and well proportioned design and among the largest or the largest that had come to this New Spain, the admiral chose it as flagship and made his [earlier] flagship the vice-admiral's flagship, dishonoring the one that had been such [by saying] that it was given to rolling. But the one that he chose gave one so great that it threw many men into the sea and only those escaped who succeeded in grabbing hold of the tackle and channels [part of the rigging] when they began falling. Six who fell directly into the sea were drowned because they did not wish to swing the vessel around to wait for the ones who were coming swimming behind it nor to put out the launch to pick them up. But all of them in time paid the penalty in the same coinage, as I will explain later.

I will tell about an entertaining ghost incident that occurred one night on a vessel, while I was on it, before the departure from port. It was the vessel belonging to Luys Sestin. And the one that gave rise to it (*envistio*), the one that they abandoned off the island of la Palma. This ship had a small fishing net. And it had taken a great deal of fish with it on the previous day, from which a good old sailor took some. And placing it in a wax (*cera*) from an earthen jar (*botijo*), he put it behind his box. And on lying down on it at night, he placed a hard ratline (*rreuenque*) over the wax of the fish, with which it was tied (*se seña*) in which he kept the key for his box tied. And a scabbard of raw leather in which he kept a butcher's knife. When everyone was asleep and when the deepest silence prevailed on the ship, a cat was attracted by the odor of the fish. And wishing to stick its head into the wax where it was, it placed it inside the loop of the ratline. On feeling itself caught, it took flight. The result was that the lasso tightened more. And leaping down below from there because it was in the little fore-castle (*castillejo*) of the prow, frightened by the noise that followed behind it from the ratline, key, and scabbard, fleeing and leaping all around the ship, there was not a man left among those who were sleeping above over whom it had not leaped. And all of them, not knowing what it might be, got up struck with terror, and some, shouting. As a result, they awakened the entire fleet. The cat, stuck in some corner, became quiet with the fright and noise of the people. With that the noise from the cat ceased and the people, although terrified, returned to their posts. But, with the silence the cat came out from where it was. However, in moving about, once it sensed the noise from the ratline, it took flight again and it was forced to make a second passage through the same areas. On entering into the stern cabin, it became wilder still. When it located the door, it went out without its wits. A sailor who saw it without knowing what it was ran after the cat, which, closely pursued, crawled in behind a hen-house, where it remained without stirring. And the sailor, who saw it enter and not come out, approached the hen-house. On not hearing any noise, believing that it was something from the other world, he said to it, in the name of God I command you to tell me who you are and what you want. Everyone was present by this time. On seeing that it neither responded nor moved, they returned to their quarters. Once things had calmed down, the cat came out anew and returned to jumping over everyone with the same noise and fright. As a consequence they arose [again] more terrified. And with the great fear, noise, and shouts, the cat, running helter-skelter, fell through a hatchway below between the decks, where the hubbub and fright were even greater among the people who were there sleeping because the darkness was greater. And with great confusion, they all rushed to come up by way of a small trap-door, where, with all pushing, each one wished to be the first one to come up above. They shouted with fear and some were saying that it had passed right over them. Others that they had touched the tail and that it had hard paws. And others that they had felt it throw itself down into the ballast. As a result of this, the fright among all of them was greater than it is possible to describe. Those from the other ships asked what was the cause for such disturbance and uproar. And no one knew what to reply.

In the midst of such confusion it was decided to light a candle and investigate whether it was something from this life that had them so terrified. And as they had to go down below for this, no one had the courage to go down alone to light it. And coming to an agreement, two went down and they lit the candle. And while searching through the corners of the ship, they found the cat very terrified, hidden between the covers (*dujas*) of a cable. The people were so terrified, as they confessed later, that if they had not seen that it had been the cat, no man would have remained on the ship, [that] everyone would have abandoned it.

The fleet remained in the port of San Juan de Ulua for almost a year waiting for the silver. It departed from the port on the second or third of July.[3] After one month of navigation, *The Crucifix* galleon remained in the sea without there having been a storm other than that one night it gave a roll (*cocollada*) and with it it cast the main yard of the foremast (*trinquete*) and bowsprit into the sea. Because of its being night and because the galleon was going then to the leeward of the entire fleet, it was luck that it was seen from the old vice-admiral's ship and by those of another vessel. We remained with it that night and the other vessel made the best use of its sails that it could until it caught up with the fleet. And everyone returned there the following day. After removing all the people from the galleon and some things of value, it remained on that sea without any other damage, nor taking on even a drop of water and, while being, as they were saying, within easy reach of Puerto Rico. It was learned later that after six months had passed, Englishmen ran across it and off-loaded the things that they found on it. In those days the flagship found five or six galleons off the cape of San Anton that were waiting to escort us. And because of their not lowering the flag, as was said, on their spotting them, as if they were enemies, they turned aft to leeward fleeing from them and the entire fleet followed their flagship. And the galleons, tired of waiting, returned to la Habana where the [other] fleet was waiting for them, all the armada and fleet from *Tierra Firme* [northern South America].[4] A storm hit our fleet and scattered it and the flagship was in great danger of being lost. It stripped a great deal of caulking from the sides. When we reassembled, it had many seams covered with cask-staves. For this reason and because of the winds being contrary, it took us sixty-two days to go from San Juan de Ulua to la Habana, something that has never happened before nor since.

When we arrived in la Habana, where the armada and *Tierra Firme* fleet were waiting for us in order to make the voyage to Spain at once, September had already begun. As the winter was about to begin, we all remained in la Habana to spend the winter. During this time, the general of the galleons sent to the one of New Spain (*al de la nueba españa*) for the silver of that year [and] to *Tierra Firme*.[5] And, in order not to see himself in another danger in his galleon like the past one, without reflecting on the fact that it was a frivolity to change flagships in each port, he once again took the one that he had abandoned and gave the galleon *San Martín* to the vice admiral, in which he was later drowned miserably with almost all his people.

During these days they brought some imprisoned men from Florida in a flyboat because they had killed their governor.[6] It was said that because he had a good part of the money employed in clothing when he was sending to New Spain for the *situado* (*acetuado*) [royal funds in Mexico transferred to Florida to meet the Crown's obligations there], he caused it to be received as payment to the soldiers with very swollen profits. They were submitted to justice in la Habana and they placed their heads on the old fort and in other areas. And they sent the one who was the leader to Spain in the vice-admiral's ship from New Spain, in which there also went a

Portuguese whom they arrested in Puebla de los Angles because he very much resembled don Antonio. Both were drowned with the rest from that galleon.

During this winter the general of the galleons received an order from his majesty about what he should do. It was not known for certain what this order was. But he published that he was being ordered that on such and such a day in March he should depart and carry the silver in the galleons and frigates and in other strong ships, the ones from the fleets that seemed appropriate to him, and that the fleets should wait with other galleons, over which don Luis Fajardo remained as general for the fleet that was in New Spain from the year before and the one that was going then from Spain to *Tierra Firme*. As a result of this he chose and indicated the ships from the fleets that were to belong to the armada and in which the silver was to go and, not without interest, because each one wished that his vessel should be the first one. All the officers of the fleet gathered on these indicated vessels and they were careened in a great hurry at great cost.

The rest of the vessel owners, on seeing that they would not be able to make a trip to the Indies that year if they did not go to Spain then, made an effort so that they might obtain a license for profit. And as the first ones achieved it easily, the rest requested them and all of them obtained them one by one. He knows that the permission had cost our vessel fifteen hundred pesos and with the obligation of carrying two horses belonging to the general along on it with two men who would care for them. The horses go between decks. And so that they do not move about nor fall, nor change their place, they place some doubled canvas girdles that catch them around the chest and stomach, and they tie them above on the ledges (*latas*) of the deck so tightly that they almost suspend their feet above the floor. They go with great security in this fashion without being able to move from their place nor be thrown.

This was one of the greatest mistakes that greed invented, because it was already time for sailing when these ones bought the license, and the vessels had been neglected and with the cargo on land like those that were awaiting the other fleets. On seeing themselves now with permission and without officers and little time, they were not able to refit the vessels appropriately for so dangerous a time and so lengthy a voyage. And this was largely responsible for so many vessels perishing and for the sea swallowing them with all their people.

The generals were blamed for all the disasters and excessive expenditures. The one of New Spain was charged with the blame for having repaired (*se envestido*) the two vessels on the second day after he departed from Cádiz, because, if he had had an order to wait for the two galleons in the port, he could have done it [properly there]. And his having abandoned the vessel later off the island of la Palma when it was possible to order it to put into port. And they would have unloaded it and fixed it, and it would have made its voyage. And of having later abandoned the galleon *Crucifix,* when it was possible to order it to go to Puerto Rico. But the greatest [fault] with which they charged him was his having retreated to leeward (*arribado*) so as not to lower the flag to the galleons, when he had to do so compulsorily [in any event] on entering into la Habana. And it was for this reason that he entered so late and obliged the armadas and two fleets to winter there. It was said that the cost of that wintering over reached two millions because everything rose in price. A pound of biscuit was worth four reales and a dozen bananas a real, when a bunch (*razimo*) was worth [no] more than a real even in the time of fleets. And all the rest of the things were valued similarly. And because of this, many sins and murders were committed, and every day there were people maimed and hanged. And two of each some days and other days more. From this delay also originated the sum of money that the other general derived from the licenses, and the cause of the loss of many vessels that were not properly prepared because of this mistake. Ordinarily, the disasters and losses that happen on the sea are of this sort, [resulting from the] greed or neglect of those who are in command.

When the time arrived, which was Saturday the eleventh of March, day of St. Eulogio, of the year of 1595, the two fleets and armada departed. No vessel at all remained behind that did not leave whether they had a license or not. The deception is most clearly evident in this, and that there had been no such order from the king. For they were not making it to be obeyed. Don Francisco Coloma was going as overall general, and as flagship, the galleon *San Filipe.* Counting galleons and frigates and other armada vessels, they all would amount to about thirty. It was said that they carried twenty-two million which, with fourteen that the other two fleets and galleons were carrying, meant that thirty-six million entered into Spain that year, because it was silver from three years. Among the vessels from New Spain were going the one that had come as vice-admiral's ship in the same fleet and brought eleven hundred tons of freight. It was named *Nra. Señora de la Merced* (*Our Lady of Mercy*), which was the one that the swordsmith built in the works of Seville. The troubles that follow happened to it.

The fifth day after we departed from la Habana, when we were already coming out of the Bahama Channel, Wednesday the fifteenth of March at two or three in the morning, the west wind began to blow, which is the one of the setting-sun and was on the stern for our voyage, which is what was desirable. But it developed such speed in increasing and the sea to swell that, when the dawn broke, all the vessels of the fleet and the armada were running with only one of the major sails (*papaygos),* each one as it [was] able to without maintaining the position and order that each one held. While going along running thus with the mainsail and foresail at half-mast, one of the vessels [carrying] silver, which was the flagship of the *Tierra Firme* [fleet], without being able to do anything else, put itself at our stern, and with its sails blocking the wind from ours, it came charging down on us with great fury and managed to place its bowsprit into our vessel on top of the stern. And if they had not made such great haste to lower their sails, we would all have perished there, and there would have been no one to tell about these troubles, neither would a Drake (? *ni jundraque*) have died (*muriera*) off Puerto Rico because of greed for the silver that this vessel was carrying. A short while after we freed ourselves from this vessel, as the wind and sea went on rising, so strong a wave came at us that, on hitting our rudder, it broke it off by the eye of the pendant [of the rudder] (*ojo del barón*). The pendant (*varón*), a piece of rope to which the rudder remains tied and fastened, leaps out [by][7] itself once in a while, as it is wont to, more because of having broken around the eye itself, in which it is held fast. It remains loose from the head and from the pendant (*barón*). And because of the degree to which the vessel was laboring because of being without a rudder (*gouernalle*), the rudder was easily pulled out and leapt from the gudgeons with only its head having remained attached to the helm. As we had lost the rudder, we began to fire off pieces at once, asking for help. But in so great a number of ships that were still going close together, there was not one that would help us or ask what our trouble was. And thus, with great affliction and tears from some who considered their death certain, we went along steering with the foremast sheets in pursuit of the other vessels constantly firing pieces asking for help. But all the rest of the vessels, each one followed their own fortune and had plenty to do in seeking their own remedy without taking notice of anyone else in such great tribulation because the storm was constantly increasing. As we saw that we could not count on human remedies, we asked God from whose hand alone we hoped for and achieved it, setting our hands to the task and our heart in the only one who could help us. And with some manning the pumps and others throwing overboard artillery, cables, anchors, hides, lumber, and boxes, and other things into the sea, others went with the foremast sheets in the hand steering the ship in pursuit of the rest so that we should not lose sight of them as long as daylight lasted.

The night came on. We found ourselves alone and surrounded by mortal anxieties because the wind and sea kept increasing continually and at the same pace the ship went on breaking up and opening; and it was taking on a great deal of water. The majority of the people were already dispirited. Our troubles increased because, as it did not have a rudder that would steer it, it gave so tremendous a pitch (*zocollada*) at nine or ten at night that the foremast and bowsprit were thrown into the sea. On [their] falling, it was necessary to cut the rigging by which the masts remained attached to the vessel. And with the blows that they were giving on the sides, they were punching holes in them. On completing the cutting of the rigging from the foremast and bowsprit and pushing them away from the vessel, it was no little [task] to find two men on it among one hundred people who had the courage to go down and cut it, because, in addition to the storm being so great, the cold was so intense that a drop of water that hit the body made it feel like a bullet had passed through it.

Once this task had been completed, it seemed to everyone that it was appropriate to cut down the main mast because, as the ship found itself without a rudder or sail that would constrain it in so violent a tempest [and as] the mast was giving such wide swings that it was completing the opening up very hastily with its weight, with the result that it was accelerating our end. After having consulted [on this], as the advice seemed good to everyone, one went over to the main mast with an axe and began to cut it. He had scarcely given it four blows when the vessel, with a great swing, threw the mast into the sea on the windward side. It was past midnight when it fell and the people were so tired from the heavy labor and so frozen from the intense cold that there was no one who had the will to go down to cut the rigging and push the masts away so that they would not punch holes in the ship with their blows. It was made more difficult because of the mast having fallen to the windward of the vessel. Everyone refused to go down for this reason. It was with difficulty that it was possible to finish the work with the two who had cut the rigging for the foremast to get them to cut this one as well because there were no others who had the courage for it, even though there were many who in the times of fair weather played the bully and pretended that they devoured men. They were the most despicable people in this circumstance and of less use than the smallest boys.

After having cut the rigging, the day dawned for us, which was Thursday, and the second one of the storm. On looking out over that wide and stormy sea, we discovered a ship athwart in the sea. With the sight of it, we forgot our troubles past and present because we thought that the vessel would come for us and take all of us aboard. And so that it would see us, we fired a piece many times, which was the only one out of the thirty-three that we were carrying that we had kept for this purpose. This ship was a flyboat (*felipote*) that had set out with the fleet and was carrying the *situado* for Florida. And a short while after we fired the piece, it raised the sail a little and disappeared, leaving us very sad and disconsolate and moreso than we had been before we saw it. With the disappearance of that ship, there disappeared also from the hearts of the valiant ones the little courage that they had earlier and, considering it certain they would die, they did not discuss any recourse at all. They turned all their attention solely to each one looking for the most secluded corner of the vessel, where they would not be found and that would serve them as a burial place. They considered death to be so certain that there was no longer captain, master, nor pilot; neither was there boatswain, nor watchman. No sailor appeared, even among the most courageous ones. All were searching for the most secret places on the ship in which to hide themselves best. By this time the ship was so open and broken and pierced in so many areas that one saw knees (*llauves*) broken even above the decks and the seams of the sides so open and their caulking washed out of them to such a degree that, when there was sun some days later, we saw it come in through the openings in the sides between decks. With this and with all the people so discouraged and depressed, what hope of rescue was it possible to have in so extensive a gulf.

This was the state of the vessel and its people, more dead than alive when God gave the ship's good purser such courage and valor that, with mettle beyond that of the general run of men, he brought together and inspired all the young people, who, because of being so, were more obedient and more apt and disposed for the work. And after having assembled them, he separated them into two fourth parts (*quartos*) and ordered that each fourth part should man the pumps for two hours, some [having assembled] on their own volition and others forcibly. And they did it with great spirit and without stopping for a moment. And it was all necessary as a great amount of water had entered into the ship. And in order to defend ourselves from the cold, which had become extraordinarily severe, he had all the clothing that there was on the vessel gathered under the quarterdeck and the people put it on and it sheltered the quarter that was resting and regathering some strength during those two hours in order to return to the work, which was very great because of its being continued day and night.

The good purser did not content himself with this effort because he knew very well that it alone by itself could not preserve our life for very long in view of the vessel's condition. And it was taking on a great deal of water. And thus, so that the launch might hold everyone and so that we might escape in it, he ordered the carpenter to try to enlarge it and to make it capacious enough for everyone. During the days that the storm lasted, he made some top-timbers and framing pieces and washboards with the intention of sawing the launch in the middle once the storm had ceased and enlarging it and raising it on the side with the washboards. The purser made great efforts during these days to encourage the uncivilized ones (*los brabos*) in the fair weather and draw them out of the places they had chosen for their burial places. And he was not able to get through to them (*acabar con ellos*). They replied to him only that they did not want to see so many souls drown. They were so fearful and beaten down by the fear of dying, that it had swallowed them already with the result that the purser would have negotiated better with them with the stick than with reasons because the dread had deprived them of reason. And it would have been the correct approach (*hubiera sido asertado*) and they would not have plotted so great an evil in their withdrawal as they committed later.

They remained buried until the fourth day. And the fifth one since the storm began was Sunday the nineteenth of March, the day of the glorious St. Joseph, and it was very clear and serene. Those who considered themselves as dead came out above. As they had tasted the fear of death, they remained so terrified that they very freely committed any crime whatever in order to see themselves off the ship. And thus it appeared to them that if the launch were to be cut apart and enlarged more time would be spent on it than that which their cowardice promised them of life. They dealt secretly with those who were in command during the time of fair weather, who also had appeared by now and began to breathe. But they did not have the courage in order to take charge. Only the purser had this. And from what appeared later I do not know whether they discussed this evil (*malda*) with him that he should say in public that the launch should not be enlarged because, the way it was and with the washboards, all of us would fit in it. But they had agreed in secret that, once the launch had been let down into the sea and the conspirators had entered it who were those who had come back from the dead, that out of the rest, who were those who, after God, had given them life, the ones who could might escape, and the rest should die. Those idle ones and false men made this arrangement in such great secrecy that the poor souls who kept themselves busy, working day and night without stopping in order to be able to keep the vessel above the water, as they never thought of committing such a betrayal, they could not understand it. Instead, they believed that everyone would fit in the washboarded launch as they were stating in public. And without guile nor resistance of any sort from these simple people, they themselves set things up for the placing of the launch on the sea. They placed a pump close to the little castle on the port side, and close to the quarterdeck a piece of the mizzen yard (*berga de la mezana*) and tackle and rigging (*vn aparejo*) on each part. And the launch on them (*en ellos*), in which they had placed some earthen jugs of wine and money and all the carpenter's tools that they found on the vessel and the lumber that the carpenter had worked during the days of storm in order to enlarge the launch and all the sets of nails that they found, and seven swords. Some sacks of biscuit and some earthen jugs of water were seen in addition to this to be put on the launch on putting it on the sea. In this one sees the evil intent of these people, for they were more interested in carrying off the tools, lumber, and nails that they had need of than the bread and water without which they would not be able to live. They were saying that they would enlarge the launch on reaching the first island.

With the things spoken of laid out and prepared, we suspended the launch and, before swinging it out from the gangway (*portalo*), some of those brave souls were already crawling into the launch. And in pushing it away from the gangway, so many were allowed to fall into it that the rigging of the prow broke and the launch fell suddenly into the sea on that end. And if they had not hastened to cut the tackle and rigging on the other end, their navigation would have terminated there. As soon as the launch fell onto the sea, and before its being secured, seven of those valiant ones took the seven swords that they had placed [there] for this [purpose], although we the simple ones did not understand it up to this point, as we saw that they were putting up a defense with them so that no one else might enter the launch other than the conspirators' group. And for this, while they were pushing away (*se desuiaban de*)[8] from the vessel, they held the points of their swords upwards so that those who jumped from the ship either would fear to [do so] or be stuck on them. But in warding them off, as they did speedily, they used slashing blows and stabs against those who were coming swimming. And if anyone managed to put his hands on the side of the launch, they struck them with axes or machetes. They wounded others in the face or head with the swords without any mercy before they got close to it, when they were able to reach them. They received and treated in this fashion those who jumped from the ship thinking that they would accept them. And thus many wounded and sound ones went about swimming among sharks, and some disappeared on drowning. That it did not appear other than that they called them, for the greater terror of the poor souls, because none appeared before this. Those of the launch showed themselves no less cruel with those who were already inside of it than [they were] with those who were swimming, because they gave a sword thrust to one of them who was corpulent and had seated himself in the prow of the launch and they threw him into the sea. We threw a board from the ship to this fellow as he went swimming for a certain distance, but he must have been mortally wounded and he was food for the many sharks that were swimming about there. [There was] another one whom they wished to throw into the sea who was seated on the floor timber of the launch, whom they called Big John and he certainly was. When they laid hands on him, he stuck his arms under the keelson. On seeing that they could not remove them, they stabbed him twenty-five times. But they must not have been [done] with the intention of killing him. And wounded thus, he was saved in the launch. I saw him later in Triana and he told me about the evil way they had treated him and the stab wounds they gave him.

Those of the launch, now tired of shedding blood, pulled away from the ship to where those who were going about swimming no [longer] bothered them so much. But wheresoever the launch went, the healthy and the wounded ones always went on following them, although in vain. After having placed the launch a good distance from the ship, they asked those of us who were on it for some sacks of biscuit and earthen jugs of water that they had left prepared and that soon all of us would enter (into the launch). But, as the simple ones who were [left] on the ship now understood their malice, although late, they replied that all of us should enter first and that the last one would give the water and biscuit. They did not accept this request because the ones who were killing and wounding the ones who were inside the launch [already] and those who were swimming in the water, would hardly receive those who were still on the ship. And because there were some on the ship [still], like the master, captain, and carpenter, whom they wished to bring, who must have been among the conspirators, and who had been negligent at the beginning in entering into the launch, and now were going about searching for an occasion for being able to take them on. And on seeing them in the galleries, it appeared to them a good opportunity to place themselves below [them] and to take them on. God blinded them so that they might not see the perceptive ones who were awaiting this opportunity. When the launch arrived below the galleries, they reckoned that they were carrying out a theft and that, without being noticed, they would be able to take on the captain, master, and carpenter. But as there were others more observant and diligent, scarcely had they placed themselves below when, from above, even though it was very high, without searching for any other way of getting down, a great many let themselves fall straight down, who took no notice that they had the points of the swords turned upwards. In a short time the launch was full of people and they had to pull away hastily, loaded with many whom they were not seeking and without the carpenter whom they so greatly wished to bring along. When they were pulling back, a poor sailor was letting himself down, whom everybody loved because of his being virtuous. He was carrying one hundred pesos tied to his belt. Thinking that the launch would come back at once to take him on, he released his grip on the rope that he had been grasping, trusting also that he was a good swimmer. But he went to the bottom at once like a stone. And it left all of us very distressed and terrified to see so good a man come to his end so quickly that we could not believe it after having seen it.

Those of the launch were still desirous of bringing the carpenter along because they were going with the intention of enlarging the launch on the first island that they encountered. And those of us who were in the ship desired that he should stay. And as he did not know how to swim and as the launch did not dare to come close to the ship, this assured us of his remaining. But, in order to make it more secure, we wished (*quejimos*)[9] to take him and tie him up. But as he was aware of it, he managed to flee. And keeping himself very quiet in a quarter of the vessel, he found a rope within his reach and arranged in such a way as if it had been prepared for that purpose and as if the launch had been signaled. Thus it arrived in an instant and in one and the same moment, he was swinging by way of the rope and the launch was receiving him. There is nothing more to be made of this than that these men, with special planning and thinking it out well ahead of time and maliciously, wanted to leave us without any human remedy, because they sought out and carried off all the carpenters' tools and sets of nails that were on the ship and even the pieces of wood for the launch that had been worked. And all without being needed. And not content with this, they persisted so pertinaciously until they succeeded in carrying off the carpenter, with the result that they would leave us completely without a human remedy. God willed that we should place all our trust only in his majesty and not in men.

When all the conspirators found themselves together in the launch, although with many more people than what they had wanted, who amounted to up to fifty-five, it seemed to them that it was not a good idea for them to leave without taking along some biscuit and water. And accordingly they asked for it with the same arguments as when they had requested it earlier. To this they were given the same response that they had been given earlier. This left those of the launch highly indignant. Very full of anger, they incited one another, saying, here we are seven men with seven swords, Let's go and kill these rogues (*vellacos*). At this time an artilleryman had aimed a piece with the intention of sending them to the bottom, but we did not permit him to fire. But so that they would not take us by surprise, we brought out a quantity of pikes, which were adequate arms for those who, with such great advantage, only wanted to defend themselves from seven swords. Those of the launch, however, became so discreet that, on seeing the pikes, they lost their anger and withdrew. And with a soft (*blanda*) voice they said to us, May God be with you and that they should do what they were able to in order to keep the ship afloat; that, on reaching the first island, we would leave the people on it and that we would return for those who remain on the ship. With that they raised the sail and disappeared in a short time. Those men were able, if they had been [true men], to return for us soon (*pudieran estos hombres si lo fueran voluer luego por nostros*), because they met with a large launch on which only seventeen men were going, who had stolen it from the galleon *San Martín*, the vice-admiral of New Spain's ship. And as they received part of the people from the launch into it, they could have received all, but they thought no more about us.

The first thing that those of us who remained on the ship did once the launch departed was to gather in the ones who were going about swimming, helping them to climb up because they were frozen and tired. And the seven of them who were wounded, we cured them with balsam. During all this tragedy the purser remained on the ship in his long linen trousers and shirt with a drawn sword in his hand. And when the carpenter had embarked on the launch, we begged him that he might remain on the ship with us. He gave his word to do so and he kept it. After having collected the people and cured the wounds, we went down below to see what water there was. We found that it had risen twelve and three-quarter feet (*vna pica*) in a little more than two hours that the demands and replies had lasted between those of the launch and those of us who were in the ship. This sight contributed a great deal to a mortal discouragement that fell over the hearts of almost all the men of age. It was not so great among the young people, although some were discouraged. With blows (*a palos*), the good purser turned to these and to the ones who were not excessively old, his heart on his chest and the soul in the body and the hands on the props (*binbaletes*) of the pumps. Because the weather was good then, we sought to remove some of the great deal of water that the ship was taking on by means of a diver (*buzo*) that the launch did not wish to take. It took some, but as they [the waters] were so great, we felt its benefit little because the ship was so shattered and coming apart at the seams that we saw the sun enter through the seams of the sides between decks. And with what was entering being so great along with what was inside the ship already, with God helping us, we set to it at the pumps with such great spirit on that day [and] continuing through the night that, when the following day dawned, we had conquered the water. This should be attributed only to God in order to become believable and not to human forces. And moreso with [our] being so weak because all of us amounted to only thirty-seven persons and some of these very much boys and one cleric and the pilot and a passenger and a caulker all hindered by their great age and discouragement. Besides these there were the seven wounded ones and others hidden because of their discouragement. That if it had not been with blows, which the purser knew how to do very well, they could not have been made to work. We were divided into two quarters. And each quarter worked at the pumps for two hours. And each pump needed at least seven men. With forces so weak against such strong and tireless contrary ones, what hearts, even though they were of diamond, would not have fainted, if God had not assisted them and strengthened them.

We were greatly encouraged soon after the departure of the launch when a sailor told us that he knew how to make a launch and that he would do so. And we believed him at once. Without further delay we assigned it to him as a task. And two of us went to the round-house (*tunbadillo*) of the rudder (*timón*) and we took it apart. And on the same day we took out a metal piece (*lata*) for the keel of the launch. And because it appeared small to us, we laid it aside (*la harrimamos*) and dismantled (*deshezimos*) part of a storeroom (*panol*), which was under the quarterdeck (*alcazar*) from whence we took out another piece of metal (*lata*). Because it seemed very fat (*gordo*) to us and on not having the wherewithal to plane it (*desbastarla*) because of the launch's having carried off the iron tools, we also put it aside (*la arrimamos*) and we searched for another one that seemed suitable to us. We summoned the sailor so that he might begin work on the launch. But he disabused us and said that he did not know how to do it and that he had said it only to cheer us up. And because there was no one then who had the courage to make a start, it was necessary to assign it (*sel lo vbe dar*). In this it should be discovered well whom all of us were who remained on the ship (? *en que se descubre bien quien eramos todos los que en la nao quedamos*). For among all of them there was not one who had the ability or the courage to make a start on the launch. And they entrusted it to a youth of a very young age and who knew nothing of that trade other than what necessity was teaching him. I seated the keel and fitted its stem and stern posts as best I knew how and was able to. In searching for and pulling out keels and in seating the keel, stem, and stern posts, we spent three days. There was an old Aragonese(?) (*arregoces*) caulker, who had remained on the ship and who was disheartened for the entire three days. And the purser and everyone dissembled with him without wanting to force him to work as was done with others, waiting for him to oblige us of his own free will. And if they said something to him once and a while, it was by begging him so that he might take courage and take charge of building the launch. But it was [the same] as talking with a dead person because he was always depressed and without any spirit (*aliento*) or sign for hoping that he would have it. But on the fourth day early in the morning he came out from under the quarterdeck where he had been, very spirited (*alentado*), and said to us: Our Lady has appeared to me this night and ordered me that I should make the launch because we are to escape in it. If the revelation was true or not, only God knows. But the result [was] the thirty of us saw it completed with the caulker himself being the one [who did it]. With this, I handed the launch-building over to him and he undid everything that I had done. He seated the keel that we had put aside as fat and over it he gave a start not to the launch but rather to a box (*caxa*), crossing some boards in the form of a cross over the keel and others raised up on this a foot high straight up (*otros en esto lebantados en alto de pie derecho*) and the boards over them. This lumber was very unsuitable for making the launch because we were taking it from the upper works (*obras muertas*) of the ship and it was fitted (*se asentaba*) without any other work [on it], because we neither had tools nor anyone who knew how to do the work. In this manner he fashioned a long box, tall and narrow. All this fastening, boards, and nails, we pulled out of the ship with a great deal of labor. And in [doing] this and in making oakum, we spent the time that we had for resting while the other quarter was working on the pump. Everything that the caulker ordered us [to do] was obeyed most punctually. But neither the care in obeying him, nor that which was had in giving him as sustenance the best that there was to be found on the ship, nor the stroking of him with words [typical] of sons to a father, nor the reminding him of the memory of the past revelation, none of this sufficed so that little by little and at each step he was returning to his former depression. And letting his shoulders fall, he was accustomed to say to us: you poor little souls, what are you working for, do you not see that you are drowned? And each time out of the many that he let himself fall in this manner, it cost us a great deal of time and work to persuade him with pleas and stroking so that he might cheer up and go forward with the project in which we had certain trust in God that all of us would be saved. Because of seeing him so depressed and without spirit, we took care not to speak with one another about the great deal of water that was entering into the ship, not even when it was besting us, in order to incite ourselves to go at the pumping work with more spirit. And if we did discuss it, it was with care so that he would not hear it. But this could scarcely be hidden from so old and experienced a sailor and who was working close to the pump, where he saw us tied to it continuously day and night without stopping. And with such good spirit; that with the great deal of water that the pump was pulling out, the pump-dale was always full and many times running over. This and seeing that the vessel was so large and so heavy and that it had, from the past and present trouble, many of the tightening wedges (*llaues*) and knees (*curbas*) split and broken and the seams of all the sides so pulled apart and open that the sun was entering through many of them between decks. And on seeing themselves alone on so extensive a sea with a few young men and some useless and depressed old ones. And such was his counsel that the spirit that he had was to surrender to the fear and to the dying without making any further effort or lengthening his life one hour more.

With our caulker being so old a sailor and in seeing and understanding that he was in such clear and evident danger of death, it was no great matter in being so depressed and in having surrendered to the fear and to the death that he considered so certain and so violent in itself. And if the evident danger did not overcome the young people similarly, nor the fear of dying, it was because of the lack of experience that there was in them and because of their not knowing how to conceive of it as it was. Whatever was the cause, the young people showed themselves invincible on this occasion against the fury of the sea, winds, and fear of dying. And they infused courage in some of the men and among those who had become discouraged. The good purser went to great pains so that, as long as they were not elderly or incapacitated, he might return their soul to their body by blows [if necessary] and he made them work. God abetted this courage of the young people and the continual diligence of the purser through the medium of a pump because of a new design never used up until then [which] the ship made in la Habana, which, in addition to the incredible surge of water that it drew out, as I have said, never let us down except on one occasion for a very short time. Nor was it necessary to prime it (? *guarneserla*) anew once (? *denque*) the one who did it had primed it, nor in the twenty-four days without stopping that we were working on it with the pump, something that must be attributed to God alone. For, measuring the water that was entering against the strength that we expended, and if sometimes it conquered us because of the weather being more severe, the increasing of our courage so that we should not become discouraged and give ourselves up, is seen clearly to be a supernatural work and from God.

One of those days, with the continual trouble of the ship, the shrouds (*orenques*)[10] of the mizzenmast came loose and the old pilot happening to be near, one of the pulleys hit him on the head and injured it badly (*lo mal descabro*). Later while he was in the stern cabin, the ship gave a roll and [threw] the poor old man against the wall with so bad a blow that it left him crippled afterward for all the rest of the days that he lived, which was for some years, even though he was so old that he had come to the Indies thirty-two times and suffered great troubles many times.

Some days before we abandoned the ship, we discovered an island on our leeward side and the wind was carrying us toward it at a good pace, and we were overjoyed with the sight of it more than it is possible to calculate. We were discussing the method that we would have to observe in order to disembark so that the undertow and the rocks should not kill us and about how we should unload some food for some time until we should build a launch from the pieces from the ship that the sea was bound to throw up on land with its tide in which we would have to go to the nearest port. And there was someone on the ship who recognized it and gave a name to it. With this the night descended while we were close to it. And although we desired to reach it, we feared that it should be at night. And so we passed [the night there] with a desire that the day should come in which we desired to see ourselves on the island. But when that so greatly desired day dawned, we recognized that it had been a phantom or a cloud that looked like an island, or that all of us with the desire that we had, had dreamed it. Our dream island having disappeared, we continued our work with the pump and proceeded with the building of the launch, although we never abandoned it no matter how many bouts of despair our old caulker suffered. And we always continued the labor day and night to keep the ship above the water until, when eighteen days had passed since the launch left, it was the will of God that we should finish the work on our launch. And at once, even though it was already late, we endeavored to place it on the sea and that everyone should embark on it and abandon the ship.

Friday the seventh of April of 1595, day of Saint Eufemia, virgin and martyr, our launch was completed during the afternoon. And with the other one having been launched on the windward side, which was the fearful one (*la de bauor*),[11] it seemed to us that it would be more advisable to launch this one on the leeward side of the sea because of that side being more sheltered and the waves having less force there. For this we moved the pump (*bonba*) over to that side and a piece of the yard of the mizzen-mast with which we had launched the first sloop. And the two apparatus having been put in place, we launched ours on the sea. But, with the wind picking up (*picando*) and the sea going choppy at the time that the launch reached the water, the ship gave a great roll and took it below (*la tomó debaxo*). In all the past troubles up to this point, I had not had any fear of being drowned. But, at that moment I believed that the end of the navigation and of life had arrived. But God was pleased to leave us on top of the water, although in a perilous state and open. Two young men entered into it at once to move it away from the ship with all haste so that it would not be taken under anew. And they put such an effort into it that it was separated from the ship entirely, which represented no less a danger than the one passed because, as the launch was much lighter than the ship, the wind and the waves moved it away from it at great speed. And the launch or box, because of the way that it was built and its poor proportions (? *mala tasa*), was so light and swift-sailing that it could not be kept on its plane but instead was giving quick rolls, now to one side and then to the other. At this moment we threw two oars that we had made from the ship to the ones on the launch, each one [made] of two poles (*espeques*) with a piece of board for the blade of the oar, which, by great good fortune they were able to take into the sloop. But, with the many rolls that it was giving, they were not able to row, nor to approach the ship; nor were they able to stay standing. And without being able to do anything else, they went on pulling away from the ship, from which we threw them a long rope tied to a piece of lumber or board, which they caught. And pulling themselves back by way of it, they managed to place themselves under the galleries of the stern from which they ballasted it with a quantity of iron shot inserted in linen pants and doublets.

On setting the sloop or box aright with the ballast, which name suits it well because of its shape, the first thing that we placed in it were two earthen jugs of water and two of biscuit, which was the sustenance that it seemed to us would suffice for the four days that the pilot had told us we would take in reaching land. And it seemed to each one that he would pass them without eating in accordance as the desire to see themselves on it was great. After the provisions, the first thing that we put in was the cleric and the pilot, who were not able to do it [for themselves] because of their great age, and the pilot less so because of being crippled also. And thus we placed both of them in slings. Soon everyone went about entering without opposition, when each one wished. And the people went on entering thus because the descent was difficult and because of the greatly disturbed state of the sea and the wind and because of the place being difficult to enter and with the sloop being crosswise and open to the sea, rain, and wind, it involved a great deal of danger. I offered to go down below decks at this time to see how much water there was in the ship. The cross timbers were covered with the water washing over them from above. When I went back up above and as I was going to embark on the sloop, I saw a sailor walking about very calmly over the quarterdeck eating bread and cheese. This fellow had said earlier that he did not want to embark in the launch but rather to make a raft and float on the sea in it until he should encounter some ship. Another old passenger was walking about, sifting through his boxes searching for papers. Another one offered four reales so that they might carry his box in the launch. I saw another one who arrived at the door of the gallery and was going to enter into the launch with a horn of punk and the rest for lighting it in his hand. And on a young fellow's arriving at the door at the same time with him, he said to him: take this and enter and put it into the sloop as I wish to be the last one who enters.

With that he retreated back inside and others went on entering. I entered when the sloop was already full of people and all seated on the floor-timbers. We were all squeezed together like paving stones with each one occupying very little space. The purser, who was our leader, was already inside, and the wind and water were increasing in strength. With that the ones who were [still] on the ship retreated inside it in order not to get wet. They esteemed life so little or they were so confident that we were going to wait for them for all the time that they might wish to tarry. But it should be understood well that they were not among the number whom God wished to set free from that danger with life. For in order not to get a little bit wet, they wished (? *quejeron*) to lose it. We remained suffering thus for a great deal of time with the launch athwart waiting for them to come out and [to see] whether they might wish to embark. But on the purser's seeing that they were not entering, neither wished to nor appeared, and the danger in which we remained, and that, perhaps, recognizing that, those of the ship had retreated in order not to place themselves in it, he said to the one who held the rope with which we were tied to the ship that he should let it go. And he did so. With the two oars that I said we had made, we went about pulling away from the ship, even though the wind sufficed for this. But, on pulling ourselves away, we recognized better that the launch was much broken up and that it was taking on a great deal of water because of the ship's having hit it below and that it was so light and swift-sailing that any movement whatever put it in danger of foundering. With this we considered ourselves as more drowned than those who were remaining on the ship. And the purser said that we should return. And we did what was possible to return to the ship and it was not possible because the wind was pushing us away from it much farther than our weak oars were able to return it. Doubting that we could reach the ship, we decided to make our voyage, allowing the wind and water to carry us for the meantime, when one of those who had remained on the ship, who was the one who gave the punk to the young man, saw that we were letting ourselves pull away from the ship, he said to the señor purser in a high and imploring voice that they should not carry us there (*no nos llevan allá*). And the purser replied: brothers, we are going as greatly drowned as you are remaining. And without making any further effort to return to the ship, we let ourselves go on pulling away from it. With that the seven who remained on the ship would remain reproaching themselves, some, their greed, others their gluttony, others their excessive (? *denaciada*) confidence, and others their negligence. For in order not to get a little bit wet, they were losing their life and would become food for sharks whom they appear to have called to both embarcations with a bell in accord as they appeared many and ferocious. In the first one there were deaths and drownings and they had something to get fat on. On this occasion, I do not know who called them, because, before the launching of the sloop there was no sign of any, but once it had been launched so many appeared that the sloop did not give a roll without them showing up at once at the side. And as soon as it rolled to the other side, they appeared there with such quickness that they seemed to be demons, if they were not such already in order to make us lose courage, and with these fears, cancel our voyage and the effort that we had made to return to the ship. It must have been due to their incitement because, if we had returned to it, none would have dared to reembark in the launch and we would all of us drown.

When we separated from the ship, the night was approaching and we soon lost sight of it with a great deal of sorrow from our hearts in considering what our companions were feeling on seeing us go and their remaining alone to become food for fishes. As soon as the night closed in, we raised one of the oars as a mast and from a cloak [made] a sail and steering the launch with the other oar, we went on sailing part of the night. And it seeming to us that it could support a sail, we took down the cloak and oar and raised the mast and put out the sail with which we had come prepared. Here we recognized more clearly that God was assisting us, on seeing that a launch or box that, when a man only moved his head, [the movement] carried it to one side or the other with its weight, would be able to sustain itself and navigate with a mast and sail as large as it was. One sees in this that this entire so protracted shipwreck was a continual miracle. Although we saw the great deal of water the launch was taking on, on purpose we did not deal with diminishing it until this moment. Because we did not have the wherewithal, it was agreed upon to break one of the earthen jars of biscuit so that the water could be removed with the pot portion of it. It was broken so poorly that they did not extract a pot piece from the entire earthen jar with which it was possible to remove the water. And we threw the whole thing into the sea. And because the biscuit got wet, we also threw it into the sea and we were left with only one earthen jar of biscuit and with the same need for diminishing the water in the sloop. God provided for this, I do not know by what path, with a little brass chamber-pot that was most useful to us during this entire navigation. We went about lowering the water with this and controlling our navigation to a greater degree than we had expected of the launch because it supported the sail very well, even though it was larger than what was needed for it and all of it was necessary (*y toda la avia menester*) in order to move it. Because of its poor design (*su mala trasa*), we also recognized then the providence that God had considered in [seeing to it] that none entered into the launch other than the thirty of us who were going in it because if only one more were to enter there would have been no possible room for him.

We were sailing during those days with a fresh and favorable wind, being guided by the oldest pilot of those times, who was carrying all the instruments that the pilots use for their navigation. When the three days had passed in which the pilot had said we would reach land, we expected to see it on the fourth day, but again we did not see it. On this day that was the fourth one since we departed from the ship, the earthen jar of biscuit was opened and the first ration was given, which would be so much biscuit with one nut and an agreed on amount of water (*auenecia de agua*), which was that of a cane-length tube of tin-plate [or possibly brass] (*vn canutillo de hoja de lata*). Thirst was not felt on this day because the hunger surpassed it and I did not drink the water. But the rest of the days it was the opposite; that the hunger was felt less and the thirst was raging. This passed for me, but it reached greater extremes for others because they felt it more. This thirst revealed to us another wonderful providence that the divine will used with us so contrary to what we were able to understand. It was the ship's having taken the sloop below and opened it up. Because with this it took on a great deal of water. And although it was troublesome for us to diminish it, our going always or ordinarily sitting on top of that water refreshed us and tempered the ardor of the thirst with the humidity that the dry flesh received through the pores. It appears thus that God arranged things in such a way that the present troubles were a remedy against those that were about to come. So we experienced it in this and other dangerous episodes (*peligrosos transes*) in which we found ourselves all through this shipwreck.

The ration that I said was given to us after having endured four days without eating went on continuing on each day. And we proceeded on our voyage with the hope that each day that dawned was the one in which we were going to discover land in accordance as we considered the pilot's promises as certain. And when we saw some pieces of wood, reeds, sedge and other things that the rivers are accustomed to put into the sea, it held out the promise that we would soon be close to land and that some large river was entering it around there and we tested (*pobauamos*) the water. Many times some were saying that it was sweet. And it did them a great deal of harm because it was from the sea and is very purgative. And this was the effect that it caused in those who drank it. When some rainstorm was building up, we desired that it should be a vigorous one in order to catch some water in our mouth or however we might be able to. And thus, when it rained some, we placed our mouth on the mast. And although what ran down was bitter because of passing over the mixture of pitch, grease, resin, and oil (*alquitran*), we sucked at it with the desire that there should be more. One night among these a great squall with a rain shower overtook us and it did not bother us that it was great. We swung around crosswise on the sea (*hechamonos de mar en traues*) and the sloop was like a rock and we waiting for the downpour to arrive with the desire of assuaging our thirst with it. But it all stopped in wind and very little water. While we were thus in the middle of the storm, our old caulker raised his voice saying: St. Elmo's fire, St. Elmo's fire (*santelmo, santelmo*). We all looked with the desire of seeing it and in the direction that he indicated, we saw a star among some clouds. The storm passed and we remained consoled on seeing [how] securely the sloop stood up against it, although we considered it as more certain that it [was] God by his means. By this time, which would be eight days after we departed from the ship, the hunger and thirst had consumed us to such a degree that all there was to be seen in us was the skin over the bones and no one had had a bowel movement (*auia escrementado*) except for those who drank water from the sea as from a river. Against the thirst the pilot taught us to drink the urines without distinguishing the ones from the others (*sin difercia vnos de otros*), but with difficulty. And they were such that it seemed that the liver (*higado*) had dissolved itself in them. As I have said, we brought two earthen jugs of water from the ship and when we seemed to be almost on the point of perishing from thirst, it seemed appropriate to double the ration. On opening the second jug it appeared to be empty and in the bottom of it a small hole through which it had been sucked. We were all surprised. I much more as the earthen jug was close to me and I had not noticed it. Neither [had] the cleric, pilot, and purser felt it, who had it close [to them]. And it was not possible to verify who was this very cunning thief when we were glued together as if we were only one body. Nor did the sloop permit one to pass from one place to another because of its being so prone to tip to one or the other side. That in order to control that [tilting], the purser soon ordered that we should use a young fellow with a large body as a mast. That he should be seated at the foot of the mast so that when he should see the sloop tilt to one side, he should throw the weight of his body in the opposite direction. And he did it all through the navigation. And merely turning one's head to one or the other side brought the sloop along after it. We were sailing in such great danger, if the hand of God had not guided us. This young man, who was a native of Chepiona and was named Diego de Vides, was the one who, during the first days, helped me to pull the lumber for the sloop from the ship and the one who worked the most in everything that came up in the line of work without ever becoming a bit discouraged. He had some large bunions on his feet that were in proportion with his body, which was very large, even though he was not very old. And he was accustomed to say as a joke that in those he resembled his mother.

Just the opposite of this fellow was a young Fleming, who held the position on the ship of sailor and artilleryman, who in order to (*par*) be such, it suffices that he was Fleming. In this fellow the flame of the hunger and thirst burned more sharply than in others during those days. And he did not find a place to sit in the entire sloop as a result of which he remained restless and put it in danger. And, although the purser and the rest reproached him, he did not quiet down, as it was not in him to be able [to do] more (? *que no deuia de poder mas*). But on seeing the danger in which he was placing everyone and that he was not mending his ways, with him moving ultimately to the prow of the sloop, the purser ordered that he be hurled into the sea so that only he alone would be drowned and not everyone because of him. He understood well when he ordered it that no one would move to carry it out as a consequence of the great weakness that existed in everyone and because it seemed cruel. But he had scarcely said it when everyone who found himself close to him laid a hand on him and he would have gone into the sea in one swoop, if he had not found something on the sloop to grasp strongly. The scant strength of those who

attempted it and his many exclamations with which he promised to mend
his ways and the pleas of the rest prevailed in his favor, and its being [the
will] of God (? *el estar de dios*) that we should all disembark together on
land in order to let it be understood how great was the hunger and thirst
that we endured and how close to the doors of death it placed us. Suffice
it to say that, thirty persons as we were, in the twelve days that the navigation in the sloop lasted, we drank one earthen jar of water and we did
not finish eating the other one of biscuit because we finished what was left
over for us on land. And that I say for myself and I can affirm it for
everyone as a result of going for so many [days] that, if we had not found
the land on that day, it would have been impossible to go on living. And it
seemed to me that, in dying at the hands of enemies so rabid as are hunger
and thirst, that that raging pain that one suffered would be bound to
continue in the other life. And as a result of seeing ourselves in such extreme need, we held a devotion in common, in addition to saying the *Hail
Holy Queen* (*salue*) daily to Our Lady and the major litanies. The rest of
the time was spent in desires of seeing the land and in recalling and in
discussing many times the foods and drinks that each one had seen or
enjoyed and about the springs and rivers of their lands. The memory of
this was no relief for us, but rather it caused us greater torment with its
desire. There was an old man among us who had passed the age of eighty.
And it was his ordinary amusement during those days to ask each one the
trade (*trato*) of the greatest profit that existed in his land. He asked about
it with such emotion that he seemed to desire that trade and showed a
desire of going [there] to have it. Each one ought to die wrapped in the
desires in which he spent his life. For he was discussing and desiring that
which in that time and at his age were impossible because of the custom
that he must have had and which had greater force in him because of their
not being suitable to his state and age.

Some remembrance of God was not lacking in the midst of such great
carelessness and a great deal [of remembrance] of the Virgin Most Pure,
and in particular, of the one of Mercy, because that was the name of the
ship by whose intercession we believed all of us received such great mercies from God, ones such as we have never heard of from a shipwreck.
That so big a ship and of such little strength and in so extensive a gulf,
alone, open, and broken into pieces with the continued storm and in such
a state that when the sun came out, it entered between decks through the

cracks in its side and without a rudder, nor any mast at all other than the mizzen-mast because of the storm's having broken all of them. And the captain, master, and pilots, who amounted to seven on the ship, the boatswain and boatswain's mate, and all the rest of the sailors, except there were two, one from the earldom (*del condado*)[12] and the other one Portuguese, all depressed and almost dead, and moreso the most fearless (*brauos*) and valiant ones, with each one seeking out a most hidden corner of the ship where death would be able to find them alone because they said they did not want to see so many souls drown. With this and with the ship open, with the water rising in it by spans (*palmos*), what hope of safety for the men to have in danger so evident if God, for the confusion of the reputed fearless ones, had not instilled courage in the ship's purser in order to assemble all the young people with whom he maintained it on top of the sea until, with the storm already abated, the fearless ones recovered some courage and, cautiously coming out of their holes, made off with the launch in accord with what they had arranged in their retreat. And well loaded with people and with other things, they departed with it, abandoning on the ship the purser and the young men who, after God, had freed them from death. For, on seeing that with so mortal a blow these few young men did not become discouraged, even after seeing that the water had risen twelve and three-quarter feet (*una pica*) in so brief a time but rather they felt encouraged to remove the water and to make a new sloop without paying any attention to the despair of the majority of the men who remained among the young people. The very same ones who were doing it saw all of this to be the work solely of God. And even though they gave thanks for this, in part this gratitude never reached the level of what they recognized was owed for so wonderful a work. And because of this forgetfulness, we have discussed so many of the things that I have spoken of, when we should have been spending the time thanking God for the greater marvel that we believed he had worked with such shipwrecked ones. I have neither heard nor read about it up until now at least.

From the tenth day of our navigation, when all of us were almost dead, there were some among us to whom it seemed that if the sloop were to be lost within sight of land or on some reefs or wild coast, that they had the strength to swim for a long time. But they were deceiving themselves as will be seen in its own time. The intention that all of us bore was to disembark on the first land that we should find, even though once we

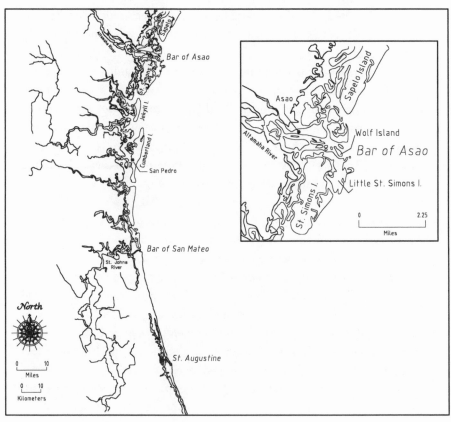

Fray Andrés's landings after the shipwreck.

landed on it, they were going to kill us with arrows and eat us. So consuming was our desire for land when we first sighted land on the twelfth day after we had departed from the ship, which was Tuesday the eighteenth of April during the morning of the day of St. Eleutherio. And we were close to it when we discovered it because of its being low. With the sight of it, the souls returned to our bodies and reviving, we gave a thousand praises to God and to the Virgin Most Pure, who had guided us and protected us in the midst of so many dangers. This joy was tempered for us with the concern that the coast should be one for which we were suited (? *ybamos enderazados*), because we now recognized that we had no strength at all and that no matter how slight the undertow might be, even if it were on a clean beach, the most of us or all of us were bound to be drowned on it.

But trusting in the Lord who had freed us from so many dangers and brought us that far, that it would not be so that we might drown on the beach but rather in order to free us, our hope did not prove to be vain because we went on drawing near to the land with this confidence. We saw that, with its being an open coast and without any shelter from the entire ocean, the beach consisted of clean sand and the sea so calm on it as if it were a small sheltered lake. And so that we might recognize more clearly to whom we owed the thanks and that it was God and not the sloop who had brought us there, with the beach being so clean that there was no grain of sand to be found on it as thick as one of wheat, and the sea, which was rising and without waves to such a degree, like a bowl of milk, when the sloop managed to touch onto the soft sand with its prow and so softly that it could scarcely be felt, it fell to one side at once as if it were tired of having sustained us for so long a time against its nature, although it had level floor-timbers like those of a box. Here all of us found ourselves thrown into the water in an instant and we recognized [that] those ones who believed that they would be able to swim for a long stretch had presumed on themselves, for they were not even able to get out of the water on all fours. And in order to encourage some of those who seemed to be stronger to help some of the older ones to get out, the purser let loose a few blows on them with the flat of the sword. If there had been any undertow, even though it was slight or if the coast had been steep, we would all have perished there. But God guided us, let him be praised for everything, to a place so good and secure.

We finally came out onto land crawling and on all fours. And the first one who reached the beach drew a cross in the sand and we all kissed it (*la vezamos*) with great joy and devotion. At once, the biscuit from the earthen jar that was left over was distributed among everyone. And each one received more than two rations like those that were given to us on the sea as I have said. The water supply had been exhausted two days before. But we were diligent in searching for it. No great effort was necessary because the merciful goodness of God provided it soon from some pools that we found close to where we landed and with a little hole that we made on the beach up to three yards away from the sea, where we found sweet and very good water. Whether this water was miraculous, God knows. What I know is that we looked for it after having found other water, although farther away. [But] we never found any that was sweet neither in that same place, nor in any other one on that beach except for the one right on the sea. Nor did the knife with which we opened the hole appear. But we missed it a great deal on having drunk, as each one quenched the fire of their thirst with very little water. Everyone's thirst assuaged, and it reawakened the fire of hunger to the point where it consumed us. Then we saw ourselves more clearly and we did not know ourselves, after having seen ourselves leave the ship so fat and robust and here so weak and dried up the way death paints one and we had only skin and bones.

It was about ten [in the morning] on the day that we set foot on land. And after moving in a little distance from the sea, we all sat down. And when it was mid-day, the pilot shot the sun with the astrolabe and told us St. Augustine was twenty leagues from there, indicating to us the coast along which we would have to travel, yonder where, to all appearances, it was twisting to the north. But directly, that path, which later turned to the east (*al oriente*) brought us [in a direction] opposite to the one where St. Augustine was and we turned our backs on it. With this account (*relacion*) and trusting in the divine providence, we tried to make our trip by land because we were afraid to reembark on the sloop. And because neither the cleric nor the pilot could take a step because of their tired [old] age and extreme weakness, and because none of us had the strength to carry them, the two of them agreed to remain there together to die consoling one another. And because there was no hope of health or sustenance for them, we brought them the sail from the launch, in which we wrapped them so that it might serve them as a shroud. And leaving them so, with their heads uncovered and without their displaying much affliction or sadness, we left them and began our march in the direction that the pilot had indicated to us. And on what feet, strength, and tramping (? *patalotaje*) we were trusting in to cover so long and hazardous a trail! And we were going along the beach like the little dogs (*gosquillos*) that, by tracing a scent and sniffing, go searching for little scraps and crumbs with which to kill their hunger. They eat everything they find even though it is rotten. We went along similarly, eating what we were finding in the way of plants or things that the sea might have thrown up on the beach and without taking notice that they were rotten. And we knew very well that some shanks and legs [were] that we found in the ebb and flow (*al rebalaje*) of rotting scraps (*sentollas podridas*). This and things like it that we were finding, we went along eating, and moving along little by little until we saw that our beach and path twisted sharply toward the north. To our right side there was a very large bay. On going forward in this manner, after a few steps we stumbled across a large pine tree [that had] fallen into the sea, with its root or stump (*sepa*) on the land from which it had been pulled up. It was already very dry and with few large branches [remaining], which left it almost sitting on the ground. As it was low tide, it was entirely uncovered. When we reached it we saw that all of it was completely clotted and covered with oysters (*ostiones*—this word denotes an oyster that is larger and coarser than the common one). And a few steps farther on there was another pine tree that had fallen into the sea in the same way and manner. When our merciful purser saw them, feeling compassion for the two old men, [whom we] wrapped up and placed in a shroud while still alive, he had us gather a quantity of oysters. And, although it was already very late and even though all of us were so badly off, he ordered two of the strongest ones to carry and bring them to them. And they did so without any show of repugnance. And they were received by them as though they were angels sent by God. We spent what was left of the day eating oysters. And after having finished off the ones of the trees, we went on forward until a little (*pequeñuelo*) arm of the sea stopped us that jutted out of that large bay and penetrated into the land, which is very level. Here we recognized that we were on an island by the special providence of God, who did not wish that anyone among all of us who had set out in that vessel (*enbarcacion*) should die in that manner. For this [purpose], his majesty had blinded us sweetly and without our suffering. For, while being able to avail ourselves of the sloop and depart from the island, it did not occur to us. And so that we might not perish of hunger and thirst, he set for us an abundant harvest of oysters, sorrel (? *azederas*),[13] and palm tree shoots, and some grasses from the beach, all foods appropriate for the weak state of our stomachs and so that we might drink, some pools of water that sufficed for the eleven days that we tarried there. This island was called Reynoso according to what we learned later.[14] It would have about one league and one-half or two leagues of circumference.[15] Its soil is level and sandy and covered with tall pines and live oaks and with palm trees like those of Andalucia. Some of our companions saw many wild pigs on it during the first days that we were there. They must have retreated when they became aware of our presence because I learned later that there was a great horde of them there. This island was unpopulated at that time and it is settled now and [has] a convent of Franciscan religious on it.[16] Because God directed our paths in such a way that in all those locations (*partes*) in which we were, settled or unsettled, belonging to the faithful or to heathens, within a few days of our presence [there] convents were established in all, which was the fruit of our [having been] lost, although it could be that their inhabitants do not see it thus.[17] But I will give the reason in its time.

The first night that we slept here, the mosquitoes bothered us a great deal. As it seemed to the purser that the sail from the sloop would protect us from it, he sent for it and they brought it, as the elderly ones would give it up with particular pleasure on seeing that by this means life was prolonged for them. And we sent them a good quantity of oysters every day and some palm shoots and water with which they sustained themselves. We missed not having a fire on which to roast the oysters for our complete relief and to chase away the mosquitoes and to warm ourselves, as we felt the cold. But God did not grant us this. And the tinder and the rest that we had brought from the ship for lighting a fire disappeared on us without our being able to find it. Although we gathered suitable sticks for lighting a fire and made every possible effort to do so and spelled one another on becoming tired, we could never achieve anything more than making it smoke because of our lack of strength or because it was not what was best for us. We saw fire at night in different locations and near to where we were. And it seemed to us that there was no other obstacle between ourselves and the fire than a small arm of the sea to which we had drawn close, of up to six or eight yards in width. We never attempted to cross it even when we were in the sloop. During the day we saw some pirogues [that] hugged the mainland shore, which was heavily forested, crossing along the other side of the bay. When they arrived parallel to us, they penetrated the mainland. We understood it to be some river, as [in fact] it was. Every time that we saw them pass by we made every effort that we could think of and that the need was teaching us in order to be seen by them, but in vain, because they never saw us or did not wish to see us.

Eight days having passed since we disembarked, it seemed to us that it would be well to make some effort to get off that island and search for the city of St. Augustine. It seemed to some that the most appropriate means was to repair the sloop, which was still where it cast us onto the beach and that we should cross in it to look for that river into which we saw the pirogues enter. If we did not find a settlement around there, we should set out along the coast in it and we would go from headland to headland down to St. Augustine in the direction the pilot had told us. The purser was of this opinion. Others were saying that they did not wish to place themselves in such danger but rather to sail around the island in search of the fires that we had seen so close at night. God was guiding both factions, although we did not realize it, because the direct path that we needed to follow and that would bring us to St. Augustine was that of the fires that we saw at night, where the chief of that village was a Christian. And there was another settlement near it where the chief and the chieftainness and some other Indians also were Christians and among them there were two or three Spaniards [posted there] by orders of the governor.[18] And thus this was the correct path. However, the will of God, as we saw later, was that we should split up for other purposes that we did not understand. And, accordingly, some left to go around the island and we, the others, left to repair the launch. The caulker going with us, we reached the spot where we had left it, and we dragged it up on land. When it was placed on some supports, the caulker began to repair it as well as he could. While it was daylight we went to our old campground for water and oysters, because we were not able to find water, as I have said, other than salt water except where we had found sweet water when we landed. And there were no oysters in that spot. When we returned loaded down, nightfall was already approaching, and I remained half-way along the path all night. And thus I was not there for the launching of the vessel in the water. But before it was fully light, they came to where they had left me. And when I had entered into it, we went to the arm of the sea that I have spoken of, and we put a quantity of oysters into it that would serve us both as ballast and as sustenance. While we were engaged in this, those who had gone to circle the island arrived without having found a crossing. And they asked the purser with a great deal of submission to forgive them and to carry them along in the sloop. The purser responded to this that it would amount to tempting God [to do so] and that it did not make sense to place everybody in danger of drowning again without need. That they should remain there and take care of the sustenance and the entertainment of the two old men. That he gave them his word that as soon as he reached any place whatever where there were people, he would do as much as he could so that they would send for them at once. With this, we split up, the landlubbers remaining unhappy and two brothers separated, one on land and the other in the launch.

Friday, the twenty-eighth of April, day of St. Vidal martyr, at nine or ten in the morning, we left the island in search of the river that we believed existed on the other side of the bay. We arrived there directly in a few hours at the mouth of the river, which was very wide. And we proceeded upriver all that day aided by the wind and the tide. We went along making landings at determined spots where we discovered that they had made a fire, but we never found anything but charcoal and ashes. In one place we found a little shallow well (*pozillo poco hondo*)[19] with bad water that harmed us when we drank it. When the tide began to run out, it seemed to us that we had already gone upriver a great [distance] without finding people or any hope of finding them. And, thus, we returned downriver with the intention of going out to sea and of going along the coast from headland to headland in search of St. Augustine. We descended until well into the night, when the tide detained us, and we anchored in the river with a stone-like anchor (*potala*) of shot placed in a pair of sailors' trousers. And we set a watch so that we would see any pirogues that might pass on the river.

That same day a short time after we left the island, that it appears that God was waiting for something else, a small pirogue arrived at it in which there were two young Indian men and an old Indian woman, mother of the head chief of the kingdom of Azao. They carried some pieces of cake (*torta*) [made] of parched corn and others made from live oak acorn flour and a lit piece of wood. They gave it all to our companions, and they in turn gave them a rosary and a little blanket and some other little things. And they gave the Indians to understand by signs how we had gone out with the sloop in search of that river. With that, the Indians departed leaving our companions consoled with the fire and the other things that they gave them. On the following day the chief of the village where we had seen the fires at night approached the island in a small pirogue within sight of our companions. He spoke the Castilian language very well and was a Christian. He pulled back at the beginning and refused to come to the shore, fearing lest we might be Englishmen, who were accustomed to mistreat them. But, having been assured that we were Spaniards, they came ashore. And on learning from him that he was the chief of that village, they asked him to carry them there and he agreed to this readily. And because the pirogue was very small, they placed the cleric and the pilot in it and the rest followed along by land. And wherever there was some arm of the sea they crossed a few at a time. And thus they brought them to the village where the Spaniards were. And they sent word to the governor at once, who, believing that there were other Spaniards lost on the coast and among the Indians, soon dispatched a brigantine (*vergantin*—a small, lateen-rigged row-sailer)[to sail] all along it with some iron tools for ransom (*rresgate*). And he dispatched a frigate (*fregata*—small vessel that was rowed as well as sailed) for us, which arrived back in the port from which it had left with a north wind that came up and the brigantine made its voyage.

Our companions were already among Christians and the two blessed old ones free, which is what it seems God intended by means of them. And we of the sloop were tied to our stone anchor in the middle of the river completely unaware of the end and happy outcome [for them]. And, concerning our trip, when it was about ten o'clock at night, which was a very fine clear one, the fellow who was on watch, who was a Fleming, but not the artilleryman, said that a pirogue was passing near there. It was news of great joy to all, as we were not sleeping, because of the lack of shelter and the poor bed. On hearing it, the purser told all of us that no one should move or raise his head. And he began to call to them in as many ways as necessity taught him, at times in Mexican of which he knew something, and at times in Spanish, telling them that we were Christians and had been shipwrecked. He repeated the cries to such an extent that they brought their pirogue over to our sloop. There were two Indian men and one Indian woman in it, and they carried a smouldering log. We asked them by sign language to go over to the bank and light a fire. A full tide was flowing, and a strong current and the bank of the river [was] very much concealed by the woods. They jumped on shore with ease and lit a fire. We reached there with more difficulty, because we had to go along jumping from one branch to another, because the bottom parts of the trees were covered with water. On arriving on shore, we saw that the fire that they had lit was one of miserly (*mesquinos*) Indians. And we soon brought big pieces of dry wood, which lay about there in abundance, and we lit a big fire, and with its light we saw our Indians more clearly and that they were carrying some things that we recognized as belonging to those who remained on the island. And asking them by signs where they had obtained them, we understood from their signs that they arrived [at the island] soon after we left it, and the rest, which has already been recounted. The Indians soon lay down to sleep with the confidence [they would have had] if they had known us for many years. And our Spaniards did the same. I did the same at the beginning, but I must have felt the pricking of hunger more and the desire to eat roast oysters. And I got up and went to and came from the beach many times as the tide kept going out until many oysters were uncovered. And I loaded up with them and set myself to roasting and eating them. Soon the rest of them began getting up. And we spent what was left of the night in roasting and eating oysters and praising God, who had given them to us without thinking about it. Before it was daylight the tide began to rise, and we embarked, we in the sloop and the Indians in their pirogue. And as they moved more swiftly and our sloop slowly, even though it was under sail, they wished to go ahead and leave us behind. We asked them that, inasmuch as they wanted to go on ahead, would one of them remain behind with us in the sloop and guide us to their land. And that the Indian woman go on in their pirogue with one of them. They agreed to this after many pleas and a male Indian entered the sloop and the [other] two disappeared very quickly. They must have reached their land shortly. We ourselves went on sailing upriver under sail all day long. That even in this God wished that we should see that He favored us. At about three or four in the afternoon we began to encounter pirogues with some things to eat for trading with us. What they brought were some pieces of corncake (*torta de mayz*) which were big and two fingers thick[20] and other yellow and red pieces of cake [made] of acorns from the live-oak (*enzina*), which were sharp-tasting and bitter and which were what they brought the most of. And we were unable to eat them. Those [made] of corn had a pleasant (?) (*lendo*)[21] taste because they were toasted. We bartered (*resgatabamos*) for this, but they had brought little of this type, and it only served to awaken our appetite and our hunger, which the oysters could not kill. With this we reached a spot where the river was somewhat narrower because the land must have been a little higher there, although it is all level. Soon we noticed a great number of Indians who were coming along the edge of the river to meet us, accompanied by a young man, a brother of the head chief of that province, whom he was sending to receive us. We in the sloop went to the shore, where the purser jumped off. He now asked us to honor him with the title of captain and all those who so desired [went] with him. They were received amicably by the young man and the rest of the leading men. And after having greeted one another without understanding each other, they all walked along upriver close to the river bank to the first village, where they were lodged in a large Indian hut (*un gran jacal*)[22] [a council-house type building] which served as royal houses. There they brought them [something] for supper because it was already night when they reached it. Those of us who remained in the sloop went upriver in it, guided by these Indians who put us in great danger of capsizing because they traveled in the launch standing up. We finally arrived at the village itself where they fed us under a tree on the riverbank after we jumped to the shore. For supper there, they brought us a very thick gruel (*atole*)[23] [made] from parched corn in some earthenware bowls (*casuelas*), roughly made (*toscas*)[24] and deep, very much like the ones the Indians in these kingdoms [New Spain] use. All those that we saw in different areas there, and some very distant from the others, are of the same workmanship. We supped on the *atole*, which they gave us without charge, and on some Castilian roosters that we bartered for. We lay down to sleep [then]. But we experienced a bad night and a worse day, because our stomachs, weak, cold, and without warmth, were not able to digest such strong food. And even though we were not able to eat much because of the weakness of our stomachs, nonetheless, with the desire that we had to kill our hunger, we ate much more than the natural heat could warm up, as we were almost consumed by the past hungers. This was one of the greatest dangers of death in which we found ourselves. And in it we recognized the mercy that God had used with us in bringing us to that island and in detaining us on it for so many days eating oysters and grasses, which was the food that our weak stomachs could then digest.

We arrived at this kingdom of Asao Saturday the twenty-ninth of April, day of St. Peter Martyr. The first thing the purser requested on the arrival of the caciques, even though it was already night, was that a large pirogue, well fitted out with the necessary provisions be dispatched to the island from which we had departed the day before and that they should bring back in it the two old men and the other companions who had remained on it. Without any protest, the caciques dispatched it shortly well stocked. So there would be no mistake in this [matter], the brother of the one who remained on the island went in the pirogue. The pirogue was there at dawn. When it did not find the people and saw the island half-burned, they returned and entered the village on the following day. Then we learned that they had been taken off, as has been stated.

When the day dawned for all of us there, many little Indian boys came early in the morning to where we of the sloop were. And, even though they were very small fellows, all brought their bows and arrows proportioned to their bodies and stature. All of them positioned themselves to shoot at the top of the tree where we had slept, chattering happily with one another without our understanding them or knowing to what purpose they were shooting there until we saw a small snake falling from the tree, its little head pierced with an arrow. One of those little boys came up very proud and, raising the pierced snake on his arrow, showed it happily to all of us as a conqueror and more skillful than the others his peers.

The clothing of the men of this province and of those who are neighbors to it is one single deerskin, very soft, not tanned, but rubbed between their hands and with their fingernails, which they never cut. The clothing of the women (*dellas*) is a sort of sack-like garment (*vna manera de gueypil*)[25] and underpetticoats (*naguas*) made from a long plant (*del pastle largo*) that grows in the trees,[26] made after the fashion of flounces (*a manera de fluecos*).[27] The *gueypil* hangs from the neck (*cuello*) to somewhat below the waist (*hasta mas de la cinta*)[28] and the petticoats from the waist to the ground. All (*todos*)[29] wear their hair long and they cut their hair a little over the forehead. They stain that part with red ochre (*almagran ellos*) along with the chest, upper arms and thighs (*moledos y moslos*). Some wear strings of beads (*abalorio*)[30] on their wrists, upper arms (*molledos*), knee (? *ligadura*)[31] and ankle (? *garganta del pie*)[32] for grandeur. All generally keep their arms and legs lean (*enjutos*) between the blood-letting place (*sangradera*—or bend of the arm) and the wrist and [between] the thighs (*molledos*)[33] and the feet (*patorrillas*). All the children that I saw had these parts bound (*señidas*) and compressed (*apretadas*) before learning to walk, which is the device they use to keep them lean (*enjugarlas*). All commonly enjoy very good health (*son muy bien dispuestos*),[34] [are] clever (*sueltos*),[35] and of very good features and limbs (*faysiones y mienbros*). Their skin tone (*color*) is like the ones of this land [Mexico], and some whiter, more so the Indian women. They are tall (*altos*—male) generally. I did not see any fat one (*ninguno gordo*); they have robust and strong limbs. In the matter of their agility, it is said that they run after the deer shooting them with arrows without losing sight of them. From what I saw of the land, which amounted to many leagues, there are no stones, and the soil, because of being so sandy, must not be good for adobes or they are not given to making them. For this [reason], all the walls of the houses are of unfinished logs (*maderos toscos*)[36] and covered with palm. They excel in putting it together (*componerla*) and in softening a deerskin (*abladar*)[37] and in hunting and fishing. All the houses are small because, as they have little to keep in them, they build them simply for their shelter. And for this [reason], the chiefs' houses are also small. The head one (*el mayor*) out of seven [caciques] that there were in this province, who was a young man of my age[38] at the time, with all being in the village where he lived, he took a liking to me as his equal in age, and took me to his house and showed it to me. It had three or four small rooms and it differed from the rest in having something more in the way of provisions. But this was nothing more than maize and some Castilian hens, and in having two women. He had them loaded down with *deerskins* in place of the common dress of Spanish moss (*pastle*). It must have been for grandeur. As for the rest, one would have covered them the same as all (*lo mesmo les cubria vno quetos*)[39] because of their wearing them one over the other. Here in these villages the river is already free of the water from the sea. Its width will be up to twenty-five yards. The water appeared to have depth. A great abundance of big catfish grow here after the fashion of those of Cuernabaca, which the Spaniards call *bocones* (big mouths), in contrast to the other small catfish that are produced on that coast in the estuaries where the rivers enter the sea. I killed (*mate*) many of them in the port and river of St. Augustine.

In this first village we remained lodged for two days in a large *jacal*, round in form, built of entire pine trees that lacked only their branches and poorly stripped of their bark. They had their foot fixed in the ground (*asentaban el pie en la tierra*)[40] and their tips were all joined together at the top like a pavilion-style tent (*pavellon*) or like the ribs of a parasol. Three hundred men would be able to sleep in it. It had all around [the wall] inside it a continuous bed made of tree branches (*tenia por de dentro todo en derredor un continuado cadalecho*)[41] or cot (*catre*) well suited for many men to rest and sleep in it. Because there was no other clothing (*rropa*) except for some straw that they threw underneath (*debajo*), the door of the *jacal* was so small, that we had to stoop down in order to enter it, made thus on purpose against the cold, which we felt when we arrived, [even] with its being summer (*verano*).[42] In order not to feel the cold of night and to sweat without clothes, it sufficed to close the doorway with a [door] (*vna*) made of palm that they kept there for this purpose and to light two firebrands (*tizones*) inside. We sweated at night with only this and on being inside we did not feel the cold of the day. They kept us here the first two days, giving us without charge and with signs of much love all the gruel (*atole*) or porridge (*poleadas*) and cakes of parched maize that we were able to eat. We bartered for the hens with things of little value and so slight that on one occasion I did not wish to give two needles for a hen. When these days had passed, the head chief wished that, for the rest of the days that we should have to remain in his kingdom, that it should be in his village, which was near. We moved to it with ease in an afternoon because the trail was very level and clean and because we did not have to move anything other than our persons. There was little more than an hour of daylight left when we arrived at the village. We found the head chief and his leading men, who were many, in a large and clean plaza at the door of a *jacal* similar to the first one in every respect, but larger. They received us with happy faces and affable expressions and words that we did not understand just as they did not understand us. They soon attempted to entertain us with a certain game. To start it off, they all assembled together in one section of the plaza together with their cacique, each one with a pole (*bara*) or a piece of a sharp-pointed lance (*asta pun-tiaguda*) of the shape (*hechura*) and size of a dart (*dardo*). One of them (*vno dellos*) did not resemble them. The chief had a stone in his hand of the shape and size of a half-real bread roll (*torta de pan de a medio real*). On beginning the game, the one who held it threw it rolling (*la arrojo rrodando*) with all his strength, and they threw their poles after the stone all at one time and without any order. They took off after them at a run at the same time. I did not understand the game very well. But it appeared to me that the one who ran the best and arrived first took his pole and the stone and, without hesitating for a moment, threw it back again in the direction from whence it had come. They took it again in the same manner and threw it once again.[43] They spent a great deal of time in this exercise and became so involved in the chase that the sweat ran from all over their bodies. Once the entertainment (*fiesta*) had ended, we all entered into the council house (*jacal*) together and we all sat down, Spaniards, chiefs, and leading men, on the bed made of tree branches (*cadalecho*), which was raised more than a yard from the ground. In the council house and close to the door on its right side, there was a little idol (*ydolillo*) or human figure badly carved. For ears it had those of a coyote and for a tail that of the coyote as well. The rest of the body was painted with red ochre. Close to the idol's feet there was a wide-mouthed jar (*tinaja de boca ancha*) full of a drink that they call *cacina* and around the jar and the idol was a great number of two-liter pots (*ollas de a dos asumbres*),[44] also full of *cacina*. Each Indian took one of these in his hand, and with reverence they went about giving it (*la*) to those who had played, who were each seated on a bench (*cadalecho*). Each one took and drank his. As a result of this their bellies became like a drum and as they went on drinking, their bellies kept on growing and swelling. They carried this on calmly for awhile, and we [were] waiting to see how that fiesta would come to an end, when we saw that, on opening their mouths with very great calmness, each one began ejecting by way of them [their mouths] a great stream of water as clear as it was when they drank it, and others, on their knees on the ground with their hands, went about spreading the water that they ejected to one side and the other. All those who did this were leading men. That solemn fiesta ended in this fashion.

They gave the name *cacina* to a little tree of the size and the appearance of the myrtle, and to make the water from it that they drink and that they call *cacina*, they toast the leaf in a deep earthenware pan (*cosuela honda*— the modern *cazuela* or stewing-pan). [When it is] well-roasted, they throw water on top of it, and while they are boiling it, they begin drawing it out and drinking it hot and go on pouring new water on top of it. Its odor is like lye-water (*como de lexia*). Indians and Spaniards drink it in the morning, and they say that it helps prevent the stone, and that because of this drink there is no Indian who has it, because it makes one urinate a lot. I drank it sometimes in the house where I was in St. Augustine, and it causes the effect that they mention, and it does not have a bad taste. But it will never serve as a real treat like chocolate. This is the common drink of Spaniards and Indians. There is no recollection of their drinking sassafras except in illness.

In order to be able to vomit (*trocar*) it, as I learned later, they mix seawater with the *cacina* with which the Indians entertained us, and they do not eat all that day until they have thrown it up. I am not entirely certain of this, because later I saw an old Christian chief called don Filipe, because he knew that was the king's name, who was accustomed to throw it up every time he drank it without its having salt water. Accordingly it may be that the vomiting of it is peculiar to the serious men among them and not [characteristic] of all.

The day following our arrival at this village, while the head chief and his leading men were together there with us, our purser asked him with brief explanations that they give us what was necessary [to get us] to St. Augustine and that they bring us there in their pirogues. [They did this] by means of an Indian that there was among them, whom they called the pilot, and who spoke some words in Castilian, although badly, and understood what was sufficient for our purposes. They responded to this shortly more with deeds than words. We soon saw the people occupied in chasing hens and grinding maize, on which they expend a great deal of effort, because they grind it in deep and narrow wooden mortars. The hand is the guide for the rammer, that is more than two yards in height, and the rammer moves upward, and the thin end in the mortar. The cakes that they make from this flour are a little smaller than *comales* [a flat earthenware pan used in Mexico for cooking maize cake], and two fingers thick. They do not make them with salt because they do not have it, and they cook them under the embers. It is very delicious bread and very nourishing. They make little of this. What they eat the most is the gruel (*atole*) and cakes [made] from acorn. The most of our provisions (*matalotaje*) was in flour, which, because it consisted of parched corn, is also eaten in powdered [form]. With the hens, cakes, and flour assembled, we went to the river to embark, where we found two very large pirogues prepared and manned [for departure]. The larger had eight rowers, the smaller one six. One of the Indians who came loaded down with hens took off with them, and although they searched for him diligently, he did not show up. As it was already becoming late, we embarked without them. The head chief and another chief embarked with us and with them some leading men and the Indian pilot as interpreter and pilot for that navigation.

Before we leave these villages behind, I will say lastly that it seems that God had [a hand] in bringing us to them. I have already told how we divided into two groups on the island, with thirteen remaining there and the sixteen of us embarking. And how the pirogue reached the island soon after we had left it. Around midnight it then ran into us, who were at the mouth of the river in the sloop waiting for the outgoing tide to go out along the coast where we had been lost, and how the Indians guided us and brought us to their villages. For these two chiefs are now embarking and going with us, and they were baptized in St. Augustine and both took the name don Martín, because the governor was named Martín de Avendaño [His name was Domingo Martínez de Avendaño].[45] After they were baptized, they asked for ministers in their land who might teach and indoctrinate them in the faith that they had received. And because there was no more than one very old cleric in all of Florida, the governor sent to la Habana to ask for religious and [some] from the order of St. Francis came on the same frigate that brought us to la Habana. This was the beginning and origin that this sacred order had in Florida.[46]

Who would think that with troubles, losses, and paths [that are] twisting and wandering from our point of view, that God was directing them toward such lofty goals as the conversion of many of those poor souls to whom nobody had paid any attention because they had neither gold nor silver.[47] And God determined our path in such a way that in all the districts where we were, both populated and unpopulated, the first five convents were established, because a Spaniard crossed over to the island where we first were and as many Indians [went] with him to establish a convent there as were suitable for his administration.[48] And thus God has gathered more fruit from these kingdoms by means of our troubles and losses than from all the expeditions the Spaniards have made in them. Father Torquemada said that the Indians of this island and those of Azao, to whom he gives another name, killed the religious one night. And from a creole from St. Augustine he learned that the Spaniards hanged our head chief don Martín[49] because of that and the Indian pilot and others. It is possible that he may have been saved by this path. And he told me that in that province the situation of the Indians has deteriorated greatly since the Spaniards entered into it.

Before we left the village, we gave the sloop and its sail and the shot that we used for ballast to the chief along with a large machete and a little axe. When the governor learned about it, he sent for the sloop and the shot, and they brought the sloop to the village of San Pedro. Two Indians, wishing to cross the river in it, capsized it, and it threw them into the middle of the river. Such was the vessel in which thirty people crossed so rough a sea with such difficult weather. We, the people and the pirogues, left Asao, as I have said, on Tuesday as the sun was setting, the second of May, the day of St. Athanasius. As dawn was breaking, we arrived at the island from which we had set out, and we found part of it burned. We made a fire there in order to lunch, and we soon left in search of St. Augustine. We traveled all that day by rivers and arms of the sea, and when it was afternoon already we sighted the village of San Pedro and with it in sight, we finally learned from our Indians that our companions were there. We reached land, because the village is on the bank of the river or arm of the sea, and before we disembarked our companions had arrived accompanied by the Spaniards whom the governor maintained there and by many Christian Indian men and women who lived there, but without mass or sacraments. They all received us one by one and embraced us with signs of love and joy and brought us to the council house (*jacal*), which was bigger than those that I have spoken of [before now], and it was open at the top with a skylight (*claraboya*) such as can be made in a council house, round in shape and [made] of whole pine trees. They gave us *atole* here for supper as the daily ration. And our purser played the giant (? *se hizo gigante*) and hid (*alsó*)[50] that they had given us in Asao. And if we ate a hen it cost us four reales. At last we ate by a set rate (*por tasa*) if we did not search for it. We tarried here for fifteen days, because, as I have said, the frigate that the governor sent for us put back into port (*arriuo*) and was not able to come until the fourteenth day and we departed from San Pedro in it on the fifteenth.

During those days that we tarried here its chief came, who had been absent. He and the chieftainness were Christians and spoke the Castilian language very well. He had a very good carriage and countenance, of great strength. He was named don Juan and dressed well in the Spanish manner. And when the chieftainness went out she wore a cloak (*manto*)[51] like a Spanish lady. When we learned that they were arriving at the riverbank, we all went to give them a welcome. All those among their vassals who learned of their coming, who were many, flocked to the same reception. On jumping on land, he took the path toward the council house once he had spoken to us and all of us with him. But the Indian men and women [and] the big and little children began as great a wailing in a high voice as if they had dropped dead before their eyes. And they went along following them thus and crying up to the council house, where he sat down on the bench made of tree branches, and all the Indians, got down on their knees before him continuing their crying, while he listened with great calmness and seriousness until, from fatigue he got up and left. And the Indians, on ceasing their crying, got back to their feet and left, drying their tears. Those who were absent because they had not been present at the reception and those from the distant villages came later. When there were many assembled, the chief came and, seated on the cot (*catre*),[52] the Indians went down on their knees before him and performed their wailing until he rose up and left. They returned to their houses. The coming to weep was continued in this manner for many days. They told us that their vassals had to do the same with our (*nros*)[53] chiefs when they returned to their land. Later, while I was in St. Augustine, I went to the river every day to fish, and from there I would hear someone begin to cry in a high voice every afternoon, and that the whole village would soon follow in the same tone. And when I asked the reason, I learned that their chief had died, and that accordingly they had to cry for a whole year. All this people cry in this manner for their chiefs living and dead.

As we were here for some period of time, we wandered over on some occasions to the other villages that were close. We saw patches of ground on the trail that, instead of being covered with grass, were covered with blackberries [that were] very short and woven together and so loaded down with berries that the ground covered by them was dappled red and black. No small number of them satisfied our need. It may be that those which the Inca said were very thorny in this kingdom are of this type.[54]

We had been in San Pedro for fourteen days when the frigate arrived and in it a little wheat flour, which the governor sent us. And that night the soldiers kneaded it and cooked it under the embers and pulled out a very good bread, because the experience they have in this has made them masters. With this we ate bread, and we took our leave of all that people, and we embarked and also our chiefs and the Indian pilot. We set out before it was daylight (*antes que fuera de dia nos partimos*),[55] and before we left this river for the sea, they showed us the site where the Frenchman had their fort, and they [the Spaniards] call it San Mateo. It will be fourteen or fifteen leagues from St. Augustine. An old soldier told me the story of how they expelled them from there.[56] Later I will tell what I remember of it. We had such wonderful weather this day, which was Friday, the 16th of May, that after having sailed twenty leagues we disembarked in St. Augustine before the prayer (*oracion*).[57] When we arrived, some officers sent by the governor were waiting for us on the pier so that they might lodge us among the soldiers. But it was a superfluous effort, because so many soldiers came to receive us that they carried us to their houses almost by force and in such haste that to the house to which I was brought, two comrades brought two of us to one house. But afterward I was so importuned by other soldiers that, when more than fifteen days had passed, I could no longer resist [and] had to ask permission of my first hosts [to move]. And it having been given, I moved my person to the other house, not having anything else to move. There were four comrades here in this second house, a sergeant and a corporal and two honorable soldiers. I was better off here than I had ever been throughout this pilgrimage, because I had food in more abundance, and I got along well with them and with my first hosts, because, as I had no other occupation, nor any obligation to ask the governor for the time of day, I spent the entire day fishing. And I was always fortunate and brought back fish for all. And so great is the kindness of the soldiers of this presidio that when I needed a canoe for the fishing, as my hosts did not have one, never did I ask a soldier for the loan of one, that he did not give it to me with signs of being happy to do so. And whenever the owner I approached needed it for himself, I asked someone else [to loan me one], and [he] gave it to me with the same good will and readiness. The majority of the soldiers of this presidio had come there shipwrecked like us, and they had forced them to remain there as soldiers. Because they had known such suffering, they understood how to feel pity.

Before leaving the first house in which I stayed, I went to fish a number of times with one of the soldiers from it. His manner of fishing was: we would go out in a canoe, and we would enter some narrow arm of the sea, such as there are on the other side of St. Augustine. When it was high tide, we would block the passage with a piece of wickerwork or stretch of reed patches that were long and close together. I remained in the canoe while he roamed at will among the reeds. As the tide began to go out, the fish began to go back out again. Many of them, and especially the mullet, as they bumped into the reed beds, jumped up over the reeds, which were more than two yards higher than the water. Some fell into the canoe and more passed from the other side, from having the canoe well-positioned (*bien desuiada*). Being engaged in this fishing, when it was already low tide and when the water in that arm was below the knee, the soldier said to me that if I wanted clams that I should get out of the canoe and gather them while he took the fish with the casting net (*tarraya*). I lowered myself into the water and in place of putting my feet on sand or mud, I put them on top of clams (*almejas*) as big as the fist, and with both hands, as if I were taking them from a pile, I threw as many as I wished into the canoe. From this abundance of clams and from what I have said about the oysters, one can gather how abundant is every type of shellfish in this land of Florida. It also abounds in every type of fish of excellent taste. More (*demas*) about the other methods that the natives have for fishing this [abundance]. They build weirs along the coast, some simply of stakes driven into the ground, and these are small. They make others bigger, which enclose an area equivalent to the reach of a musket-shot, out of stakes and reed grass, all driven into the ground and well-tied together, placed in line (*en ala*) in the manner in which one would make a sweepnet (*chinchorro*).[58] And in the middle between the two arms, where it is the deepest they make a small enclosure (*corral*) where the fish collect (*se recoje*) when the tide goes out. And they catch them with a casting net.

This soldier, with whom I went fishing sometimes, was among those who had been at that presidio the longest. They had removed him from his post as sergeant, not because of any fault in his person, because with it [his person] and as a man (*en honbre*), he could fill any post whatsoever. This fellow told me about various events that had occurred in that land. He told me that in years past the king had two presidios on that coast; this one of St. Augustine and the other in Santa Elena, sixty leagues distant. There were no more than 150 soldiers in each one. During this time the French established the fortress of San Mateo, which he said [was] twelve or fifteen leagues from St. Augustine. In it he [the Frenchman] had 600 men and some warships with which he set out to rob those who came up through the [Bahama] channel and sailed along that coast. The Indians could never become reconciled with them, and they sought continuously to ambush them, and when they came out from the fort, they shot them with arrows. For this [reason] and because they did not have water within the fort, at night a Frenchman placed himself on a little ass. The Spaniards were not unaware of any of this as more experienced in the land and more in contact with the natives.[59] It happened that with Pedro Meléndes Marquéz being there, who was adelantado of Florida,[60] the French went out with their ships to rob as they were accustomed to, and he [the French-man] brought half of his people out in them, and he left the other half to guard the fortress, with a nephew of his who led them. A few days after the ships went out, there was a great storm at sea, and Pedro Meléndes who knew that coast well and took pride in being an astrologer, believed that, in accord with the spot in which it could have caught them, they would have been wrecked inescapably and thrown onto the coast, from which would issue the people who escaped from the ships.[61] And without delaying any longer or waiting for any other evidence, he took the people that he could withdraw from the 150 soldiers who belonged to the presidio, and with this [force] and with great secrecy reached San Mateo and went to the place which the Frenchman with his little ass frequented for water. Having captured him, he learned everything from him that he wanted to know concerning the fort. And giving the ass with the water to one who understood the French language and having instructed him well concerning what the other fellow did and said when he reached the gate so that they would open it to him, the new water-drawer (*asacan*) and pre-tended Frenchman reached the gate and called out and the careless gate-keeper, without recognizing the voice in opening the gate, received his recompense with his death. Pedro Melendez, entering into the fort with his people, fell upon the unprepared Frenchmen, and when the dawn came there were none of them alive. And reassembling his people, he marched to seize the passage (*paso*) of a river where he believed the Frenchman (*el frases*) would have to come inescapably to cross if he had become shipwrecked with his people, where and how he was imagining [that he had]. And it happened thus that, having been stranded on the coast with his ships, they made it to land and were walking to their fort (*fuerza*) like shipwrecked, hunger-stricken, and disarmed men. Having reached the river under these conditions, they found that Pedro Melendez Marqués was waiting for them on the other side with his people at the ready to defend the crossing. To terrify the hungry and disarmed French-men more, he told them how he had already left all their Frenchmen dead in the fort and [the fort] destroyed. And so that they would believe it, he showed them a hat belonging to the young governor as a piece known to them. With the sight of this, they became certain that he had destroyed and killed them. They surrendered unconditionally to Pedro Melendez, who refused to grant any quarter to the many who begged him for it. And not being in a position to do anything else they surrendered to him. And he, as to heretics and fugitives from their king, which it is said they were, did not spare the life of more than one sole [man], who was a Catholic and a good surgeon. I made the acquaintance of this [fellow] in St. Augustine. He was then a man of forty years of age and of a very good personality and behavior. He treated our pilot, and as he was very old, he did not get well. This was the end that the French in Florida experienced.

This soldier also told me in addition: that always when they went out armed, it was to punish some crime that some villages or kingdom had committed against the Spaniards. They did so at night and with so much secrecy that they had already received the blow before they saw from whence it came. For this [purpose] they had a brigantine and a frigate in which they were accustomed to embark at night with full secrecy. And because the majority of the villages of that land are near either rivers or the arms of the sea, they disembark near the village at night and the soldiers spread all through it, and at the same moment each one in his area sets fire and keeps a watch at the doors of the houses that are burning so that the ones who are inside will not come out. And once they feel that many Indians are assembling, they withdraw to their vessels where they defend themselves with their arquebuses, and they return to their garrison, leaving many behind them burned and dead. They have all of them fearful, held in check and oppressed with these assaults. And that the reason why the Indians of Asao received and entertained us so well was, because the Indians had killed a soldier while he was passing through these villages, whom the governor had sent that he might go up to Santa Elena by way of the coastline to look for shipwrecked people on it. The image or human figure that was in the council house was the figure of this Spaniard, made to scorn him and placed there [by] the Indians. Fearing that the governor was going to punish them for this crime, burning them for sure, it seemed to them that their receiving us well and entertaining us offered them a good occasion and means for overcoming the governor's displeasure. But [to me] the manner in which they received us, treated us and entertained us and of going along with us and being baptized did not appear to arise from fear but rather from love of the people and of their faith.

The city and fort of St. Augustine were established on an open slope (*ladera llana*), unobstructed to the east at the edge of an entirely clean river. It would be about one-half league wide and one [league] distant from the coast of the sea. Its soil is sandy, and the earth in it so loose that even a very shallow well will not find support in it. Those which they have in all the houses, they line with barrels, one on top of the other up to three or four, because the water is not deep. It is sweet in all the wells, even though the seawater enters into the river. All the walls of the houses are of wood and the roofs of palm and the more important ones of plank. The fortress is [made] of wood backed by a rampart (*terraplenada*). They told me that now they have made a little apartment in the middle of it of lime and stone brought in at great cost in order to protect the powder in it. All the residents of this city are soldiers, and the majority bachelors (*solteros*). Those who are born here, who are few, if they have the strength to fire an arquebus, are given a position as a soldier. There are very few Spanish women, and I only heard it said that one Spaniard was married with an Indian chieftainness. The roster of this presidio is three hundred, and God ordained that when we went there, it was completely filled, and they lacked only an artilleryman. They turned to our Flemish artilleryman for this [post]. He excused himself by saying that the other Fleming was a better gunner, and the other said that it was because he was not that he came as a sailor. The governor, on seeing so great a contest in humility, ordered that both should stay on. They remained [thus], along with another young man [who was] a gunsmith, because the one who was there was old, and the governor insisted that the one who was young should remain to succeed him in that trade. I saw some grape vines [*paras*] and fig trees in this city, and they produce well. They also produce good melons and watermelons and pumpkins and other vegetables in abundance. They ship onions from here to la Habana even though they are not very large. There are some villages of Christian Indians a quarter league and a half league distant from this presidio and some or the most speak the Castilian language well and dress in the Spanish manner. There is a small island on the other side of the river covered (? *polada*)[62] with trees and palms, and there are a few cows on it belonging to the king. There are no others in all the land. Many very large cypresses (*sauinas*)[63] grow on the banks of the rivers from which the Indians make large pirogues. On the outside they simply remove the bark from them and to excavate them on the inside the aforementioned soldier told me they hollow them out with fire. This would be before they had contact with Spaniards when they did not have

iron tools. Now [only] those [use fire] who do not have it [i.e., such con-
tact], because the pirogues that I saw appeared to have been worked with
iron tools. The Spaniards make the walls of their houses out of this wood
of cypress (*sauino*) because the part of it that is in the ground does not rot.

We spent thirty days in St. Augustine supported at the expense of the
king because, as soon as we arrived, the governor ordered that we be given
a ration at the king's expense just like the soldiers. At that time there was
only flour, and they gave a pound and a half of this as a ration each day.
Later there was jerked beef, of which we also were given a ration. Our
hosts collected it all, freeing us from this chore. They also kneaded the
bread and cooked the food. That they know how to do all of it well, and
they did it with great charity. When they gave us passage, the governor
ordered that they should give each one of us an arroba [twenty-five
pounds] of flour and a good quantity of jerky, and our hosts turned it into
biscuit. When I went to say goodbye to my first hosts, I discovered that
they had prepared another similar quantity of biscuit and jerky from their
flour so I had to bring a double portion with me, in which there is revealed
the great charity that this people has.

Having said goodbye to our hosts, we embarked on the king's frigate
that had brought us from San Pedro and that was now going to la Habana
for the *situado* and to drop us off there. On its return voyage, in addition
to the subsidy, it was to bring the religious of St. Francis who gave a
beginning to the foundation of that province. Eight soldiers, who also
performed the duty of sailors, and the treasurer and the pilot and a
Biscayan youth embarked on the frigate in addition to our companions.
We left port on Saturday the 17th of June. We made this whole voyage
always staying along the coast from headland to headland without getting
half a league away from it [the land]. When the wind failed or was contrary, we jumped on shore and towed the frigate with a line, and we proceeded in this way. Four soldiers serving as an escort went along a little
more to landward with their arquebuses. From the time we left the port,
pirogues [full] of Indians were constantly coming out to meet us with
things to trade. All of them had as many people as they would hold. They
all paddled standing up with long paddles (*canaletes*)[64] two yards [in
length]. The blades (*palas*) were a little over five inches (*una sezma*)[65] wide
and half a yard long and the handle like a lance, all well worked from one
piece of strong (*rezia*)[66] wood. They always set out long before we reached

the coast opposite them. When they did not set out in time to catch the frigate before it passed, and when they fell behind us because the wind was strong, they would shout, saying, "amayna, amayna, toltuga,[67] toltuga, pescado, pescado, zanbo, zanlo"[68] ("Lower the sails, lower the sails, turtle, turtle, fish, fish, amber, amber"), and although we never waited for them, their pirogues were so swift (*ligeras*)[69] that by dint of rowing they always overtook us. Once they boarded the frigate one needed to keep a watch on their hands because they would steal whatever they could, and they had no shame about being caught in the theft. They bartered the fish that they brought for glass beads (*abalorio*) and things of little value, such as needles and thread, and for the amber with knives, scissors (? *dijeras*),[70] machetes, axes, and mirrors. They [the Indians] tricked some, giving them disguised resin (*piciete mascado*)[71] as amber, which looks like it. I heard it said in St. Augustine that the governor paid them twenty-two ducats an ounce for that which the soldiers brought to him. These Spaniards laugh at those who say that the amber is the excrement of the whales, and they say that it never appears on the beach except when the sea is greatly stirred up by a storm. They consider it certain that it grows on the sea floor and that with the movement that the waves cause on it, pushed by strong winds, they stir it up and pull it up and cast it on the beach, where, if they delay in gathering it as soon as it appears, the birds eat it. The Indians, aware of this, flock to the beach in the morning to search for it when there has been a storm.

I did not see any village at all along this coast, but only hamlets (*rancherias*). They say that the villages are farther inland. When we were short of water we gave the earthen jars to the Indians of these hamlets so that they might bring it. In one of these [hamlets] I noticed that when the Indians saw the arquebuses, they went down on their knees and with their hands crossed, trembling they said, "*miedo, miedo*" ("fear, fear"). In another, after having given them the jars, we all went along with them in a troop. I noticed that one of them drew apart [from the rest] and took off by another trail. Believing that he was making off with the jar, I set off after him, which brought me out to where the Indian women were hidden, and, when they saw me they let out such loud shouts, that the soldiers [also] shouted to me that I should break off [my pursuit] and come to where they were. I heard the shouts over some very beautiful trees at whose feet I was. They must have been cypresses (*sabinos*),[72] although I did not take note if they were. A beautiful and very clear lake was surrounded by these trees. There must have been some large springs that were feeding it, and these trees were the only thing around the pond, which encircled it and beautified it. Beyond it, all the land appeared [to be] sand clear of woods. Early in the morning one day we arrived at a hut where there was a pot (*casuela*) placed at the fire with mullet as whole as God created them. I noted that they all were wounded in the little fin (*aletilla*) that they have in the middle of their back. They wound them there with a thin pointed stick like a little harpoon stuck in a rod (*vara*), and they are so skilled that they do not miss (? *no hierran*)[73] the fin at which they aimed, because it must be better to grasp it there than at any other point.

All the Indians of this coast wear nothing more than a breechclout woven (? *dexido*) of palm of the width of four fingers[74] with three strands (*vamales*). Two of them circle (*señen*) the waist and the other [goes] below and each one ends (*remata*) in a tassel (*borla*) of the same palm. All three together form a broom (*excoba*) that covers part of their buttocks. In some districts of this coast I saw a great quantity of the spine bones of the whales which the Indians kill. They told us that they kill them with a stake and a mallet (*maso*). All that coast is a continuous sand bank of little depth and all along it many fish. It must be for this reason that many whales come on to it to eat. When the Indians see them they go out in their little canoes, and the first who reaches one jumps on top of it with the stake and the mallet (*mazo*) in his hand. Even though the whale might wish to sound very deeply, it cannot, and after touching the bottom it turns upward again, and the Indian who rides on top concentrates solely on fixing the stake in its breathing hole, which they do quickly. They leave it thus and return to shore, where the sea casts it [once it has] drowned. There they cut it up and make jerky for their food supply. Those of the interior in particular use (*los gastan los de la tierra adentro*)[75] a lot of it. These Indians neither sow nor gather, nor do they have any more concern about their food or their clothing than the animals and the birds, and [yet] they do not lack anything, and live to be very old, happy with their lot. On this coast, near the place they call cape of canaverales (strand of reeds), there are some Indians whom they call of Xega. They are considered to be inhumane, cruel, and enemies of Spaniards. We saw none of these, nor did we go on shore in their land. And near the land of la Habana, almost in a direct line from the port, there are other Indians very friendly toward the

Spaniards whose cacique at that time was a don Luis. The soldiers said about him that he had been in Spain. He spoke the Castilian language as well as if he had been brought up at court. I believe that it was he of whom the Inca said that he killed the priests of the company [Jesuits], because the name, the language, and the land make one believe so.[76] This chief came out to meet us in a large canoe, made in the Spanish fashion (*labrada a lo español*), with sixteen rowers, all rowing standing up, and he placed in the poop, also standing up. On reaching the frigate, he came aboard it, and he was received by all the Spaniards as a great friend of all of them, which he was. His clothing was what nature gave him, to which he added a breech-clout. He stood out from the rest in the spirit and the nobleness of his person and in the respect that they all showed to him, and in the many beads with which he adorned his body, circling with strings [that were] four or six fingers wide his throat, upper arms (*molledos*), wrists, below the knees (*debajode las rodillas*), ankles (*gargantas de los pies*),[77] above the ankles (*ensima de los tobillos*). In this [way] the king distinguished himself from his vassals. This chief brought more amber than all those who came out to us all along the coast. When he had done his business and taken his leave of us so fluently (*tan ladino*)[78] and amicably, he entered into his canoe. Standing positioned above the stern, he began to head toward land, and after a few feet he was pitched into the sea. When he had managed to get back into the canoe, he went for one of the rowers, and seizing him by the hair tossed him into the sea. He went to the bottom at once, and the cacique, taking hold of his oar raised it above his shoulder with both hands. He remained waiting thus for the Indian to come up to the surface that he might hit him with it, and, tired of waiting for him and of our seeing him armed in this fashion, he let go of the oar and went to his seat, and the Indian soon appeared above the water and entered into the canoe. They went on, leaving us amazed that a man could remain under the water for so great a time without drowning himself. With this example, it is no longer difficult [to understand] how they leap onto the whale and go down and come up with him until they have driven the stake into him.

When people are traveling along this coast, some Indians bring sets of ships' nails and some pieces of sail to barter. Somewhat farther along in the trip we encountered a ship we recognized as from our fleet from New Spain [the fleet in which he was shipwrecked] called *La Escorcelana*. It was in one piece. That because the sea floor was clean, it must have been its weight alone that took out the bottom. We learned that its people had had some fights with the Indians, and that, having made a boat, they had gone in it to la Habana, which was close to there.

On the eve of St. Peter and Paul, Marcos de Aranbulo entered into la Habana with the silver from Peru.[79] Before entering, he discovered two English ships near the port and sent two frigates after them that were larger than galleys. They carried plenty of people and each one six half-culverins of bronze and so swift that in twenty-four hours, they covered 100 leagues. As the English saw themselves being followed by enemies so strong, they fled to hide themselves on the coast of Florida, which they had nearby. The admiral's ship, which saw them take that route, fired a piece [for them] to reassemble. The frigates, which without a doubt would have overtaken and captured the pirate ships, let them go on and returned. However, the English with the fear that they carried with them went on heading for the coast. We, finding ourselves at the same time in the crossing and straight above la Habana, cut loose from the coast. A little farther on a soldier said: a ship off our prow. And soon after they said: they are two English ships. We turned back toward land. We encountered a thin spit of land like a defensive trench (*albarrada*) which the sea entered within for some leagues, and it had some mouths at open stretches like broken bridges. We passed to the other side by one of these as it appeared to us that the English ships would not be able to pass over. But farther down he found another wider and deeper mouth through which he passed. With this we found ourselves far from the land and pressed by the enemy, and with a lack of wind. That as it lessened, the enemy closed on us, and as it picked up we pulled away from him. The reason was that the frigate had three sails and they six. Nonetheless one of the ships never overtook us. And if our treasurer had been a man, as were the few soldiers, or if he had not been captain, they had the spirit and the courage to attack and take both Englishmen rather than to flee. And they were given a very good opportunity because, as the wind slacked off for us, their lead-ship overtook us while the other one remained very far away. And situated on our stern, it began firing its cannon at us and shouting, "Lower the sails, lower the sails." But the eight impatient soldiers did not want to do anything other than to prepare themselves not only for defense but also for attack. And for this [purpose] they wanted we shipwrecked ones, who

did not have any arms to go down below decks, and they would assault
the lead-ship before the other ship could join forces with it. For this [pur-
pose] they had loaded a little swivel-gun that was carried on the frigate,
and so great was their determination, in addition to some of them being
very much men, they went on with their intention because of their great
displeasure that the enemy should rob them of their pittance, which they
[the soldiers] were carrying to invest. But the more their spirits rose and
the more disposed to attack the enemy, the more the treasurer shouted for
them to strike the sails. And he insisted on this to such a degree that, while
they were fighting the vessels (? *las barcas*),[80] without being able to do
anything else, they struck the sails and agreed, however late, to becoming
prisoner, as they had not been permitted to defend themselves open-
facedly [or] to conquer the enemy. When they struck the sails, the Englishman ordered them to anchor, and they did. At once he sent a launch to ask
for the arms, and they gave them to him. Shortly after receiving them, the
English captain, who was named Francisco Rrangel,[81] came to the frigate
and said to its people in the Castilian tongue, which he spoke very well,
"Gentlemen, he who has a good suit and two good shirts, put them on.
Leave the rest of the clothing for my people, because I have taken an oath
not to leave Spaniards naked because of the good treatment that they gave
me the five years don Francisco Coloma held (?) (*trujo*) me on the galleys
of Lisbon." By this time the soldiers had descended below by the hatchway, and they were given knives so that each one, after approaching his
Englishman, might kill him. They were so unfortunate that an Englishman saw them, who appealed to the rest at the top of his voice that they
should hurry down at once with their arms, and they caught them with the
stolen goods in their hands, which they could not deny. They seized hold
of a Galician, who was a man of action and sent him to their captain,
swearing by the life of the queen that they were going to hang him. This
uproar calmed down, and recognizing in the countenance and the gestures
of the Spaniards how sorry they were about having obeyed the treasurer
and surrendered, he said to them, if they would like to fight, let us fight. If
they had found themselves with their arms in their hands as their enemies
had theirs, they would not have said that in vain, and they would never
have dared to say that, because they recognized in them that that is what
they desired. At once they searched for the gold, silver, and amber that
there were on the frigate. He distributed the people of the frigate between

his ships, and he gave clothing and moneys to some of the shipwrecked ones. They returned the clothing to their owners who asked for it. With this the captain went to his ships, leaving a sufficient crew on the frigate. On the following day, which was that of St. Peter, when dawn came, he [the captain] returned to the frigate. On entering it, he said, "Gentlemen, this past night I have spoken with my books, and they have told me that there are so many gold chains and so much money on the frigate. Let them give them to me. That they do not want me to become rough with them." The chains were in the sea tied with a tow rope to the gudgeons of the rudder, and they pulled them out along with some money, and they were given to them. Later they all learned who the book was, that he was married in St. Augustine, and that his father-in-law was one of the soldiers. And the book, being unable to deny it, excused himself on the grounds that they had made him drunk, and that he did not know what he said. After the Englishman made this second search on the frigate, he returned all the people to it, and, leaving us the provisions that would suffice to la Habana, he left and said to us, "You will now go to la Habana, saying that the English have captured you and, on seeing you so well dressed, they will say it is not possible." With this he left the frigate to us, and we set out at about ten in the day. The same day, on the twenty-ninth of June, the day of St. Peter and St. Paul, we reached la Habana, the Ave Maria having been tolled [sometime after 6:00 p.m.], having spent 111 days on our pilgrimage after having departed from la Habana on the 11th of March of the year 1595. We disembarked in the morning of the following day. We found that some of those who had come in the first launch were waiting for us on the beach. That they were stunned to see us, because when they reached la Habana, they wished to force them to return in a ship to search for us. They had excused themselves, saying that the ship had gone down before their eyes, but with our appearance their lie was revealed. One of them took us to his lodgings and fed us bread and plantains.

During the wintering of the fleets, the captain had written about our lost ship to the swordsmith, its owner, who was in Seville, that his ship was missing some rigging and provisions. He [the swordsmith], from the wood left over [from the building] of his ship (*nao*) had built [another] vessel or frigate. (The swordsmith) embarked in it (Seville) with what was needed for his vessel (*nao*) and had set out for la Habana. But on reaching the Canaries, the English captured him and, stripping him of everything that he brought with him, cast him on shore. There he embarked on another ship. On arriving at la Habana, having been robbed by the English, he met the captain of his *nao* there and the rest of the people who got off on the first launch with certain news of his lost ship. He mourned this news about their troubles as he must have grieved over it. But when we arrived, and he saw us and spoke to us, the good man kicked his feet in the air and said that his *nao* was a very good one and that we had let it go down. But that if he himself had found himself on it, he would have been the first to wish to leave it and to save his life in whatever way he could. How much better it would have been to be there in its calmness and relaxation. For God had given him the wherewithal to pass his life. That having made him the owner of a *nao*, he should lose it altogether at one time.

The two equerries of the general had escaped with us and, wishing to be reconciled with don Luis Fajardo, they gave him an account of how the king had sustained us and brought us there at his expense. They themselves came looking for us at the orders of the general and brought us together into his presence. He ordered us that, as his majesty had sustained us and brought us, that we should serve him in that armada. The majority did not obey him. I did not have the courage for so much, and I embarked in a known vessel which was that of the *Alboroto del Gato* (Cry of the Cat) and was of the armada.

The channel that they call of Bahama, as many know, is an arm of the sea which thrusts into the ocean from the Mexican gulf between the island of Cuba and from a point to north of it that juts out from the land of Florida.[82] The channel runs from west to east between these two lands, somewhat twisted toward the east northeast, leaving the land of Florida to the north, where, in going out and much of the rest, its coast turns right. It runs from this coast by way of the ocean to the north northeast, which is between the north and the northeast. Traveling from this point of land that forms Florida, where the channel terminates into the ocean, toward the west one enters the Mexican gulf by the channel. And if one travels by land from this point some leagues to the north, the trail turns to the west and heads directly for New Spain and very close to the coast. The crossing from the land of Florida to la Habana is so short that we did it in ten hours, and from St. Augustine until we arrived at that point, which is the closest crossing to the port of la Habana and the freest of the currents of the channel, eleven days.

In all this coast, from St. Augustine down to this spot, the surf from the sea makes no more noise than does the Guadalquivir on the sandy beach (*el arenal*) of Seville.[83] The reason for this is that all that coast is level land and free of rock. That same flatness and absence of rock characterizes the land for some leagues inland and, in many places, the sea [extends] inland. And if one pays close attention, he will see that what they call a sound (*sonda*) is a point of this flat land which thrusts itself into the sea in that area. For this [reason] they cross it when they come from Spain and when they go to la Habana. Because of this great flatness and cleanness and slight depth [of water], which all that coast has for some leagues away from the land, the surf does not break and the surf of the sea does not make any noise on the coast. I can attest to what has been said [here] because I have traveled along all that coast, at times by sea, at times, from headland to headland, and at times by land. And to what the Inca said in his history of Florida, that in some places a good distance from the coast they hear the noise of the sea, and that, while hearing it, they are not able to reach it. That they saw some stone enclosures (*corrales de piedra*) in the sea that the Indians had made, in which they caught a great quantity of fish. And to other points of the course of the history, and concerning the part where they finally came out, which inescapably, even though they do not say so, has to be the Gulf of Mexico, and very close to this kingdom [New Spain]. From all this one gathers with clear evidence that every time that the [Inca's] history says that they heard the sea, [or] that they arrived close to the coast, [or] that they were on it, it was within the Gulf of Mexico. And, thus, [in] the entire trip that Hernando de Soto made from the time that he landed on the soil of Florida, even though he sometimes turned toward the north, he was always moving closer to New Spain, because none of these signs are found on the coast of the ocean, and even less on the coast of the [Bahama] channel. In addition there are other reasons that convince one that they never saw the ocean in all their trip, because if they had come out on to it, they would have left many traces and reports of themselves among the Indians where they passed in those parts, where, a few years later, the presidios of St. Augustine and Santa Elena were established, and by the tracks that they left, those Spaniards would have extracted all the story of the trail that Hernando de Soto followed. The complete absence of this report in those parts assures that Soto never went so far up. When they want to say that, when they were going in directly from these coasts (*que quando yban en derecho destas costas*), they went so far into the hinterland that he did not see them (las— the coasts) nor did he arrive at them. But to say this would be to make false history, which places him many times on the coast before they had entered into the interior and after they had entered. In addition to which, the fame of such new people would have run among the Indians from ones to the others, and when, nevertheless, they want [to say] that he has passed in those districts of the north, inescapably, it has to be by approaching New France. And the river by which they departed in the boats, would have to run to the ocean from those districts. And if they had exited there in such poorly cut boats, made without a plan or a template by someone who did not know what he was doing, and out of green, unfinished and poorly worked wood, they would all perish instead of hunger and thirst and exhaustion from traveling on the sea before they managed to reach the land of New Spain where they did reach it, because such heavy and poorly made boats would cover five leagues each day at the most, even if they were under sail and oar. They would not be able to endure this (*sufrir*) so long a time and they would travel much less, because they were accustomed to stop on shore each day. From all that has been said, one gathers that the path that those boats followed could not be a third of what the Inca said, and that if they were to search for this river with diligence, they would find it very close to New Spain. And it would be possible for him, to find it by sailing over to New Mexico or near to it as the land is so level, because it is not very doubtful that those large and abrupt freshets (*auenidas*) which that river has, without its raining, should be from the snows that melt in New Mexico with the mild weather. It is already established (*sercificarse ya*) that this is so, if the rivers of New Mexico run from the northeast to the southeast to empty into the sea. With this I have completed [the account of my] shipwreck and Florida [experience], and I return to telling about the rest of the ships of the fleet and of the armada.

It has been stated already how the galleon *San Martín*, which was coming from New Spain as flagship, was lost. Only the boatswain's mate, who was Italian, escaped from it and sixteen persons who made off (*se alsaron*) with the launch, in which more than one hundred could have gone. All the rest were drowned. A just punishment from God, because, the year before, when they could have saved six men whom the flagship pitched into the sea with a roll, it allowed them to drown because of not swinging around in the sea and waiting for those who were coming in pursuit of it and shouting. The sea swallowed other ships with all their people. The English took others because, according to what Francisco Rrangel told us, the queen had sent a large armada to wait for the silver. He assured us that it was so large that, even though the *San Filipe* went among its protectors, it would not be powerful enough to defend it from being taken. But God disposed matters so that, although many of the silver ships and even the galleon *San Filipe* itself saw themselves in great dangers, none was lost, nor did the English take [any]. Although [it was] not what they might have desired, they all entered different ports. Among the silver ships, the one that found itself in the greatest perils was the flagship of the mainland (*Tierra-Firme*) fleet, which, shortly after it separated from our vessel, sprung its main mast and pitched it into the sea and, [though] damaged (*maltratada*) it was able to put into Puerto Rico in the company of another vessel that also had lost its main mast. They soon knew in Spain of its putting into port, because the silver has wings. It is said that this vessel was carrying two million. On the frigates' arrival in Spain, they unloaded them and dispatched them at once for the silver of this vessel that had put into port at Puerto Rico. And if our vessel had been carrying silver, the silver would not have been lost with the effort that we made; nor would any person have been drowned (*se ahoara*), because, they would have sent ships for it and for us rather than abandoning it, because the silver makes fortune-tellers (*adiuinos*). The day that the frigates entered into Puerto Rico, when they had arrived within sight of it, they discovered a small English vessel and, as they were going empty and well armed and were swift (*ligeros*) vessels, they pursued it and took it, a thing they do only on rare occasions, because they do not encourage the silver ships to fight. After having taken it and subjecting its people to questioning under torture, they confessed and indicated with a finger that, behind that point, the English armada, whose admiral (*general*) is Juan Draque (John Drake), is anchored, whom the scent of the silver also had brought there. He had hidden there in order to put into port suddenly and take the silver before being detected. With this account, without awaiting anything more or reconnoitering the enemy, they put into the port and gave an account to the admiral and to the rest about what they had learned from those Englishmen whom they had taken off the port. And at once without further delay, they agreed that they would close the channel and entrance to the port with the flagship and with the other vessel (*nao*) and with two of the frigates. And after having knocked a hole in the bottom of them, they sank them quickly in the entrance in order to block it for the enemy. They placed the silver in the fort and they placed themselves on a defensive footing with it and the three frigates. They had scarcely made these arrangements when the enemy revealed himself and attacked the port. As those who were in it were prepared, they resisted it bravely. And after the enemy had done as much as he was able to and knew how to in order to enter it and take it, he withdrew when it was already evening (*tarde*) and anchored close to land. Like someone who had no one to fear, he made arrangements for a dinner that night, which was for him with his captains, who had joined him on his flagship. With poor forethought, in order to be seen and to see on what they were dining, they placed a lighted candle over the table, with the result that they revealed themselves to those on land. They, not wishing to lose so good an opportunity, an artilleryman who was there as *ayamonte* fired a piece and with such good aim that one John Drake, its admiral (*general*), was among those whom he cleared from the table. With his death, they weighed anchors on the following day and disappeared. Ours placed the silver on the three frigates that they had left and they introduced it into Spain with all the people. With this no silver at all was lost from those unfortunate fleets.

Don Luys Fajardo sailed from la Habana during the same year of 1595 as admiral of the galleons, having waited there with his galleons since don Francisco Coloma departed the past March to the two fleets of New Spain and *Tierra Firme*. It was said that fourteen million were going in that armada and fleets. As a result thirty-six million entered into Spain that year from the Indies. These two fleets and galleons arrived in Spain in safety all together. And from the better ones among these vessels and from some among those that escaped from the other fleets, a great fleet was put together for [going to] New Spain. The following year, when they were already loaded, they all assembled in the bay of Cádiz. When they were ready for departure, there also entered into the bay the galleons *San Filipe*, which was the royal flagship of the Castilian squadron, and the *San Andrés,* its vice-admiral's ship, and *Santo Tomás,* which was one of the twelve apostles of that time, and the three frigates, which escaped from Puerto Rico. These were from the destroyed armada. The galleon *San*

*Matias,* royal flagship of the squadron of Portugal, was also with them, which was the biggest and the most beautiful of the galleons that were there. There were another two Italian galleons in the company of these, also of the armada for the king. All of these were on the point of departing without knowing to where. In addition to this, there was the flagship and vice admiral's ship of the armada of the fleet, which was among the richest and the best vessels that had crossed over to this land. They were all [ready] for departure when, on the eve of St. Peter and Paul in the afternoon of the year of 1596, on the same day and at the same hour that the year before the English had taken us, a ship arrived in Cádiz saying that they should get ready because the English were coming down on it with an armada of one hundred and sixty sails. As soon as the news arrived, it was proclaimed on that same afternoon that all the people of the armada and fleet should report to their ships under the penalty of death. In response to this many were saying that the news was false and that they were feigning it in order to assemble the people to the galleons, which were ready for departure. They all embarked that afternoon and on the following day, which was the one of Sts. Peter and Paul, when dawn broke they saw a large armada from their ships, which were [still] in the bay over off the island of Cádiz. As a result, the report was seen to be true. The armada was coming invading the bay and when it arrived at the mouth and saw that it was occupied by so many and by such large ships, it did not dare to enter and anchored between Santa Catalina and Las Puercas. On that day nineteen galleys were poorly fitted out (*se mal armaron*) and sailed out from the port of Santa María. They tied up off Las Puercas, a cannon shot from the enemy, and the eleven armada vessels that were anchored among those of the fleet weighed their anchors and approached the enemy and tied up between it and the fleet. They remained thus all that day without making any demonstration other than having an artillery piece fired from the galleons without a ball. The enemy replied with another one with a ball. From the galleys they tested whether their midship cannons (*cañones de crujia*) would reach the enemy and they did not reach them and those of the enemy reached them either because of better powder or because of being set higher or because of [being] bigger.

There was no admiral in the galleons but only a leader (*cabo*),[84] who performed that role (*representaua este nombre*) and they said that he was a mulatto. The admiral of the fleet was not able to command in the presence of this one. But if he were [up] to it (? *si el fuera para ello*), he would have made up for his deficiencies (? *supliera sus faltas*), although he disliked [doing] so (*le pesara*) because necessity required it. But there was no sound; nor was the name of anyone heard in the act of commanding or of directing and ordering what should be observed for resisting and blocking the enemy's entrance. The vice-admiral's ship for the fleet, who also was such for the armada and [who], it appeared, was going to be the fiercest one (? *el mas vrioso*) on this occasion, did not appear. Don Martín de Padilla had been admiral of the galleys, whom the English feared. They had removed him and given the *garas* [possibly meant to be *varas* or emblem of authority] to another. And the latter as general of the royal armada could have commanded and ordered what needed to be done, but this fellow also did not appear; nor was his name heard; nor must he have embarked on his flagship because, while the galleys were off Las Puercas, it volunteered (*se ofreció*) to arrive at the camp (? *real*) and it did not see an admiral, nor hear his name. Nor later, on two or three occasions when the royal [galley] (? *la real*) arrived at our vessel, neither did I see him or hear him named. Rather it appears that the one who was in charge and commanding it was the head pilot. The president of the House of Trade (*contratación*) had come to Seville on that occasion for the dispatch of the fleet. But he also gave no orders; nor did he command anything. For Cádiz's *corregidor*, who was the captain and governor of the city, could know little about war and, as was said later, and most certainly falsely, that he brought the English. Pedro del Castillo also was living in Cádiz, a venerable old man who attended to the dispatch of the fleets. Among all these heads there was no one who gave any signs on the sea about what was [? to be done]; nor a tongue that would at least order the vessels that they should be quiet (*quedas*) and that each one should maintain its place. That with this alone the enemy might have given up (*se voluiera*) or not have entered on that day. And so many people would have entered into the city that with it, it would be possible to equip the fleet with so many people and militiamen (? *millicion*) that it would surpass the enemy with its forces. But they blinded themselves so that they made no effort; nor did they speak any word. They left it to each one to conduct himself as seemed best to him in accord with his whim. And as they all desired to divert the danger away from their persons and property, on the setting of the sun, as it began to be night, a small little ship weighed anchor, which did not belong to the fleet and went to the anchorage (?) (*puntal*). As the rest of the vessels saw that there was no one who would prevent it, they all went about weighing anchor one by one and entered into the anchorage where they all anchored with no one from the fleet remaining. When dawn broke on the following day and the galleons and galleys were seen to be alone and abandoned by the fleet and the rest of the vessels that were in the bay, when they should have ordered them to return to their posts, they also weighed their anchors and withdrew to the anchorage. When the enemy saw that they were leaving the entrance and bay unoccupied, and recognizing from so thoughtless a retreat that all that armada and the multitude of us was without anyone in charge who might direct it, it now considered victory to be certain, which had been doubtful up to then. Weighing their anchors, they took off after them. This withdrawal of the galleons [was not done] so much to turn away from the enemy as much as it was [done] as a result of bad advice that it went to withdraw to the point as to a narrower place where they planned to tie themselves up crosswise in order to fire on the enemy better and be assisted at the same time by the artillery from the city. But it is said of the city's artillery that it was mounted on rotten carriages, which fell apart at the first shot and that others were spiked. And thus no artillery was fired from the city and the galleons did not manage to tie up in view of the speed with which the enemy followed them. The two royal vice-admiral's ships ran aground on the beach that the sea forms in front of the anchorage towards the island's vineyards. The flagship *San Filipe* tied up somewhat better and broadside thus [it] and a frigate were fighting with the entire English armada, which was moving through the bay under sail and with one following the others, all were firing their artillery at it. And the flagship did not make poor use of its own. That as the enemies were so many, no ball missed a mark. We saw that with one of them, one of the enemy's flagships blew up in an instant. That it did nothing more than provide a blaze of fire and disappear with the sea swallowing it because the ball hit the powder magazine and it blew up with its people. This galleon and the frigate kept defending themselves and attacking for half the day without anyone nor all the power of the enemy daring to board them. And its people having grounded it, they set fire to it and they went about abandoning it while it was burning. The galleon *San Filipe* had this end after having gained great trophies from the English. That this was not the least of what it would have achieved if there had been someone to provide direction on this occasion, because, if this one defended itself alone from all the enemy's power during all the time that it was able to fire its guns, if all the galleys and fleet had been together in one place that they had taken, not only would they defend themselves, but also the enemy would lack the courage to attack the two galleons that went aground. With the haste that their people applied in fleeing, they did not remember to set fire to them. The English pulled them off and they appeared within their armada as two large mountains within little woods.

The fleet was not sleeping during this time because, on seeing that the enemy was weighing anchor in pursuit of the galleons, without awaiting further order, because there was none other than that which each one wished to impose on itself, all the fleet that was anchored in the anchorage weighed anchor at once and each one put himself in flight with the greatest haste that was possible, moving along, moving along (*sic*) to the Cádiz navyyard (*a la carraca*), which is a little inlet (*ensenada*) that is formed in the mouth of the river from the bridge. They were going in such a pell-mell fashion that, on losing the channel, they went aground for moments. Because of its being mud, they did not rip the bottoms out and as the tide rose, they went about getting out, although some remained stuck. The one in which (I) went set itself down with such willingness that, if the royal galley had not arrived because of certain contact, and others because of its command, and pulled us out, we would have remained mired there. All the vessels of the fleet arrived in the Cádiz navyyard and the galleon *Santo Tomás* and the two frigates and other vessels of the armada. Everyone was going so eagerly to avoid facing the enemy, that some threw themselves into the water to escape by swimming without tying up the ships or without considering the difficulties of the ground where they jumped off, which was swampy. The more diligent ones made off with the sloops (*chalupas*). Our vessel had two sloops. Because of this and because its owner was present, no one jumped into the water. But, fearing that others would occupy them, all of us entered into them and we took some of those who were swimming and placed them on land, which was very close. And some of ours, on seeing themselves on it [the land], did not wish to reembark. There were some who preferred to go naked rather than reembark. In a short time there was not a man among all the vessels. All disappeared and the galleys went about departing by way of Santi Petre, although, before [this], the royal [galley] came to our vessel and we put some large boxes on it that the captain said were his. From all that great fleet, only these were liberated.

Once the galleys had gone, we found ourselves alone. But soon we saw that another vessel, which was from Cádiz, had its owner present on it, and that a dozen men remained with him. And, although so few, we remained quietly in that abandoned fleet without fear that the enemy would be able to attack us. Although we saw some small tugs (*charruas*) and other small ships under sail come toward us many times, we did not fear them. Neither did they have the courage to come to reconnoiter the fleet. Nor did they ever arrive because they had no way of knowing whether the people had abandoned it. And, in the place where it was, it could be defended from many enemies. And thus we remained [there] three days without knowing what had happened in the city. We saw only a great deal of quiet in the enemy armada and some smoke in the city. On the second day the vice-admiral (*almirante*) of the fleet came to the vessels, by chance, with the intention of burning it. As he found us in it, he took some people from our vessel and from the other one and occupied them in I do not know what task. As a result he left it (*la*) very disgusted and he went off. He returned the following day and occupied the people in sinking two large vessels in the channel, which were empty, with the intention, according to what he said, of placing artillery on them to defend the entry and passage against the enemy and to defend the fleet. The people remained so disgusted with this that, after his going [again], all of us went that night and we abandoned the fleet without a single man remaining on it, which was, perhaps, what the good vice-admiral intended, because, as soon as the fleet found itself all alone that night, he set fire to it. With this, all that armada and fleets were destroyed, which it appears God had brought together there, bringing them from areas so distant, after having (*abiento*) to make such different voyages so that they might all be consumed together in so few hours. These fleets and armada came to this end after God had freed them from such great troubles and dangers from the sea. The vice-admiral who set the fire had been flag commander (? *cabo de bandera*) of the flagship of some vessels of the armada, in which he had carried out a sufficiently bloody action, protecting his own person from the danger. Later he was vice-admiral in galleons. In this post (*oficio*) I saw him (*le vi*) in an action not thought out as the office required. And it was as his admiral was entering into the bay of Cádiz, who was coming from

the Indies with his flagship, he made a salute to the city, as is the custom
and they did not reply to him. The admiral was justly miffed over this and
immediately dispatched a tender (*falua*) to the vice-admiral to order him
that he should not make a salute to the city. He recognized the disposition
(*conosiale el vmor*), because what had happened sufficed for him to ac-
knowledge the attention (*darse por entendido*) as everyone among those
of the armada and fleets understood it. But, on seeing that the tender was
approaching, before it had entered into the bay, he had all the artillery and
musquetry fired altogether. Those who keep men of such actions in such
posts are not promised any lesser indiscretions than the ones that this man
committed in burning the fleet and seven vessels of the armada, where,
with a few people, they could have defended it from all the power in the
world, in addition to its being able to be assisted by land and by sea
without the enemy being able to block it.

During the night during which we departed from the fleet, leaving it
alone because of the annoyances from the vice-admiral, we went by sea to
Puerto Real [where] there was an alarm as soon as we arrived. Some men
were going about through the streets shouting with a great din, saying, to
the beach, Spaniards, to the beach, the enemy is coming on land, this is [a
matter of] honor (*vna homrra*), Spaniards, this is a matter of honor (*vna
honrra*). It was low tide then and, because of this, it was impossible for the
enemy to be able to attack by way of there, because the sea then remained
so low and without [any depth] of water there for almost two leagues that
even a little skiff [that was] empty would not be able to sail. And it would
be impossible for him to come on foot because of the amount of mud and
holes [filled] with water. Thus it was said that those who were shouting
were thieves who intended to rob the village once its inhabitants had fled
or, on their going out to the beach to defend the entrance against the
enemy. Having recognized their wicked intent, the village calmed down
and we remained in it during that night to sleep. We left when day came
and, when we reached the royal road that comes out of Cádiz, we saw that
it was entirely filled with people of every sort and age. The men were
going barefoot with worthless and torn clothes in the English fashion and
half-yard long sombreros similar to the clothes covered their heads. Some
of the men carried children in their arms and the women with their entire
body clothed in the Spanish manner, but with poor and mean clothing,
what sufficed to cover them modestly. Some of these women carried one

child at the breast and another by the hand and other bigger ones in front
of or behind them. We learned from them that they had been thrown out
of the city in that fashion on the afternoon of the day before, which was
some hours before we had abandoned the fleet. Some were traveling in
this way to Xeres de la Frontera[85] and others to Medina Sidonia, each one
to where he had relatives or friends. We learned then about how the enemy had entered into the city, which was, as soon as they saw the galleon
*San Filipe* burning. They approached the point, forming a gangway with
their ships, scuttling the smaller ones close to land. Six hundred muske-
teers landed quickly over them. Other pikemen and harquebusiers would
go also with their admiral and marched to the city, where there was a
rivalry between its mayor (*corregidor*) and that of another city over who
was in charge. It would be for its own people, which was a mistake
(*desacierto*), [rather] than for the (*la*) [people] of the city. It also was said
that, when many of the outsiders, not having arms, asked the *corregidor*
for them, he required a bondsman for them. Under other circumstances,
that would have been proper. At this moment the news arrived that the
enemy was coming marching overland with an army and the *corregidor*,
on bad terms with the one from the city and poorly advised and ignorant
of the difference that exists between a musket and a lance, set out very full
of pride to win serious honor with his mounted people without any more
defense than their shields or offensive arms other than the lances. Accordingly, in the first shower of missiles from the muskets, they availed themselves of the feet of their horses. With the enemy already very close and
with the door in the wall not having been closed because the people on
horseback had begun to enter, the result was that, on finding themselves
now mixed in with the enemy, they all entered together, and among the
few who there were in the scant resistance that there was against the English at the gate to the city, one was its general, who was said to be a
barbarous and cruel man and that he had inflicted great insults, cruelties,
and deaths on the people of the city. But, with this one dead, the Count de
Leste became general, who as an enemy, was very humane with everyone.[86] He ordered that the women should be treated with complete de-
cency. He sent the nuns with great secrecy and a guard to the port of Santa
María. And he did not do as much damage in the city as he could have,
although they burned some of its churches and houses and others in the
vineyards of the island. Here I saw one of the houses, tower, and wine-

cellar, where they had not done any damage at all to anything. The reason was said [to be] that among the Englishmen who came there, one had served Filipe Boquin, which, I believe, was the name of the owner of the wine-cellar and house, [who] was already deceased at that time. But his wife was living. Because of this respect, this fellow, while being captain, asked the rest of them, if he did not so order them, that they not do any damage there. This case and the one that happened with us with Francisco Rrangel show the gratitude of these people well, even while being heretics. The English remained in Cádiz for nineteen days during which they celebrated and played bulls. After carrying off everything that they found in the city down to the smallest little piece of iron and other metal and after having burned everything made of wood that existed in the city, they left. All the city's people, who had scattered, soon returned to it. And the city could be seen in a short time very much as it had been before the enemy entered it and sacked it and burned it in such exterior matters as trade, houses, and stores, and all the rest. In this example of Cádiz and in that of our frigate one discovers very well with how much truth it is said that the army of sheep is stronger when the captain is a lion than the army of lions when the captain is a sheep, because each one infuses his spirit in his followers whom he leads, and, how justly the glory of victory is attributed to the captain. And that these ones who took Cádiz did not deserve the glory because they had not conquered an army, armada, or city commanded by a captain, but rather a disordered anarchic town without a head or a government.

# Translator's Notes by John H. Hann

1. A reader suggested that this ship "was probably the *San Crucifijo de Burgos,* a 600-ton galleon whose owner and master was Pedro de Madariaga." See Huguette and Pierre Chaunu, *Seville et L'Atlantique* [Seville and the Atlantic] (Paris: Libraire Armand Colin, 1955), 8 vols. in 10 1955–59, Tome III, *Le Trafic, 1561 à 1595,* 510–11.

2. I have assumed this was meant to be *patache,* which the Real Academia Española's *Diccionario de la Lengua Española* [Dictionary of the Spanish language], 20th ed., 2 tomes (Madrid, 1984), defines as a vessel that formerly belonged to the war-vessel category and served in the squadrons for carrying reports, reconnoitering the coasts, and protecting port entrances but found today only in the merchant marine. Timoteo O'Scanlon, in *Diccionario Marítimo Español* [Spanish maritime dictionary] (Madrid: Museo Naval, 1974), described it as a two-masted vessel, noting that it could also signify a small vessel used in the service of other vessels.

3. Chaunu and Chaunu (*Seville et L'Atlantique,* 556–57) placed the fleet's departure from San Juan de Ulua on 14 July 1594, eleven days later than did Fray Andrés's account. I believe this eleven-day discrepancy resulted from Andres's remembering or recording that event in accord with the Julian calendar as the Gregorian calendar had been introduced only twelve years earlier, in 1582. A reader remarked that the fleet's ships entered Havana on August 14, noting that the Chaunus confirm Fray Andrés's account of the fate of the *San Crucifijo,* observing that the *San Crucifijo de Burgos* was abandoned "off the southwest coast of Florida, before arriving at the Tortugas."

4. This alludes to the convoyed fleet system for controlling commerce between Spain and its New World possessions, which was regularized by Pedro Menéndez de Avilés in the 1560s. Two separate fleets sailed from Spain each year in the spring and summer. The first one, known as the New Spain Fleet, sailed for Mexico, with a few of its ships destined for Caribbean islands and Honduras peeling off once the fleet reached the lesser Antilles. The second fleet, known as "The Galleons" or *Tierra Firme* Fleet, headed for Cartagena. Once Peru's viceroy was alerted about its arrival and dispatched ships to Panama's west coast, the *Tierra Firme* Fleet sailed for Panama's east coast. Once both fleets had disposed of their goods and taken on treasure from Mexico and northern South America, both fleets rendez-

voused at Havana to sail to Spain together in order to enhance their security. See John Edwin Fagg, *Latin America: A General History,* 2d ed. (London: Collier-Macmillan Limited, 1969), 188–89.

5. The exact sense of this very elliptic statement is not clear. But it is evident that the purpose was to collect the treasure that normally would have gone on the following year's fleet and to ship it to Spain on this overwintering fleet.

6. As I noted in my Introduction, this alludes to the soldiers' deposition and imprisonment of Governor Gutierre de Miranda. The only published reference to this event I have found occurs in Amy Bushnell's listing of Florida's governors and acting governors; see Amy Bushnell, *The King's Coffer: Proprietors of the Spanish Florida Treasury, 1565–1702* (Gainesville: University of Florida Press, 1981), 141. In that appendix she notes: "Gutierre de Miranda (deposed by mutiny)" and "Francisco de Salazar (arrested)," but she provides no additional details in the body of her work.

7. Genaro García, in *Dos Antiguas Relaciones de la Florida* (1902), has added the "by" or "por" in Spanish, placing it within parentheses to indicate that it does not appear in Fray Andrés's manuscript. I have followed his example as the addition makes sense in this context, but I shall place brackets around such intrusions.

8. Genaro García, ibid., 167, has *descuiaban.* It is *desuiaban* in Fray Andrés's manuscript.

9. García, ibid., 169, rendered this as *quegimos.* Quejimos undoubtedly was meant to be the modern form *quisimos.*

10. *Obenques* is the modern form of "the *orenques*" used by Fray Andrés. García, ibid., 174, changed the *lo orenques* of the manuscript of Fray Andrés to *los orenques.*

11. I am assuming that *bauor* was meant to be the modern *pavor* meaning *dread.*

12. A reader suggested that *condado* "refers to that part of lower Andalusia between Sevilla and Huelva called the *Condado,* built around the properties of the Counts of Niebla." It is probably the modern Palma del Condado located in the region.

13. I have assumed that *azederas* was meant to be the modern *acedaras,* meaning sorrel or another such sour-tasting plant.

14. To date I have not encountered the name *Reynoso* being used by any other Spaniard of this period to designate such a feature.

15. Based on these dimensions for this island where Andrés and his companions first landed along with other details that appear in the account, John E. Worth, a reader of the manuscript, suggested that the island might be "the little island at the mouth of the Altamaha River between Sapelo and Little St. Simons Island, which was and is unpopulated" and is now known as Wolf Island. He also suggested that it might be Little St. Simons Island itself. Either one is more compatible with the dimensions that Fray Andrés gave for the island than is the friar's remark that not long after his stay there the island became the site of a mission. The islands that

became mission sites, such as St. Simons Island or Sapelo Island, are considerably larger than Fray Andrés's Reynoso Island.

16. An important consideration in interpreting this remark is resolving whether the "now" of Andrés's statement means 1595 or the later era when he penned the manuscript held by the University of Texas at Austin's library. I believe it probably refers to 1595. In any event, Fray Andrés seems to have erred in identifying the small island where he first landed as the site of a future mission. As Worth indicated, the only island mission in existence in 1595 that fits Andrés's scenario is Ospo or Ospogue, which he places on "the southern portion of Sapelo Island." The Asao mission, located later on St. Simons Island, was still located on the Altamaha River mainland as late as 1604 when the governor visited it.

17. Fray Andrés seems to have been carried away by his idea that "God directed our paths in such a way that" convents were established in all the places along the Georgia coast through which he and his shipmates passed within a few days of their presence there. Most perplexing is his failure to notice the existence of a convent at San Pedro Mocama on Cumberland Island where Fray Baltasar López had been working since 1587 and possibly as early as 1585. On stopping at San Pedro in 1588, Juan Menéndez Marquéz noted the existence of a church there and that many of the natives had been baptized already. See Eugenio Ruidíaz y Caravia, *La Florida: Su Conquista y Colonización por Pedro Menéndez de Avilés* (Florida: Its conquest and colonization by Pedro Menéndez de Avilés), 2 vols. (Madrid: Imp. Fund. Y Fab. De Tintas de los Hijos de J.A. García, 1893), 2: 497.

18. The statements that Andrés makes in this sentence and the one that precedes it are among the most puzzling ones in his account of the island where he landed and its surroundings. The assertions that the chief of the village in which they saw the fires at night was a Christian and that "there was another settlement near it where the chief and the chieftainness and some other Indians also were Christians and among them were two or three Spaniards [posted there] by orders of the governor" seem to be applicable only to Cumberland Island's Mocama in this era. Andrés himself later (on p. 70 of this book) identifies San Pedro as the place where the soldiers were stationed. But Cumberland Island is far to the south of the mouth of the Altamaha. If it was only long after the events that Fray Andrés first wrote an account of these experiences, his memory may have telescoped some of these details, thereby distorting them somewhat.

19. John Worth suggested substituting *spring* for *well* because *well* implies human construction. *Spring* is a possibility, but I have chosen *well* as it is the primary meaning of *pozo,* and a hole dug a short distance from the river does not seem to be out of the question.

20. One finger is about 1/48 of a Spanish yard or *vara,* or about .687 inches, giving the corn-cake a thickness of about one and one-half inches.

21. The form *lendo* does not exist in modern Spanish. Conceivably Fray Andrés's *lendo* is a variant of the modern adjective *lindo* meaning "beautiful" or "nice" or of the present participle of *lenir* meaning "to soften, mollify, or assuage."

22. *Jacal* is a hispanicized Mexican word derived from *xacalli*. Florida Spaniards usually spelled the word as *chacal*. In seventeenth-century Florida, *chacal* was used most frequently to identify a native official whose duties were similar to those of the Spanish fiscal. The chacal often was an assistant to the native's *iniha*.

23. *Atole* is a term used in Mexico and Cuba for a gruel made by boiling maize flour in water or milk.

24. Tosca could be rendered also as *thick* or *coarse* or *unpolished* or *crude*.

25. This is *quayapil* or *quayapin* in modern New World Spanish. It is a loose Indian dress for women.

26. *Pastle* does not appear in modern dictionaries, but was probably derived from *pastar*, meaning *to graze*. Spanish moss is the plant it refers to here.

27. *Flecos* is the more common form. It can also mean "fringe" or "raveled edge of cloth."

28. *Cinta* here could be rendered also as *girdle* or *belt*. In view of its being matched with *cuello*, its rendition as *waist* seems to be preferable.

29. Use of the masculine form of *todos* suggests that *all* includes men and women. Other sources indicate that long hair prevailed among both sexes, although women's hair probably was longer.

30. *Abalorio* can have the specific meaning of *glass bead*.

31. My dictionaries do not list any body part among the meanings of *ligadura*, but as *garter* is a meaning of *liga*, that usage suggests the "thigh" just above the knee.

32. *Instep* is one of the meanings of *garganta del pie*, but the instep would not seem to be a comfortable place to wear beads if one were walking about, unless one had a very high arch.

33. While *molledos* typically means *upper arm*, its sense in the context of Fray Andrés's description may mean *thigh*, suggesting that it was the calf of the leg that was kept thin.

34. *Bien dispuestos* could be rendered also as *well disposed* or *comely*.

35. *Sueltos* could be rendered also in this context as *free spirits, unrestrained, swift, bold,* or *voluble*.

36. *Maderos toscos* here could be rendered also as *thick logs*.

37. *Abladar* was probably meant to be the modern *ablandar*, meaning *to soften*. N is the letter that Fray Andrés seems to have suppressed most frequently.

38. The future Fray Andrés was only seventeen or eighteen years old in 1595.

39. *Quetos* here was meant to be *que todos*, presenting another example of the suppression of letters in certain words.

40. The Spanish text here could be interpreted to mean that the pines were simply bent over and tied together with their roots still in the ground or that they were merely laid against each other in some sense, with their bases buried in the ground in the manner of poles of a giant tepee. It could be rendered also as "they had their foot placed on the ground."

41. *Cadalecho* has the sense of a bed woven of tree branches used in the huts of Andalucia and other areas (*Dictionary of the Spanish Language*).

42. Actually it was only about a month into spring as it was about the end of April when they left the island. It probably still could be quite cool at that time, particularly close to and with a breeze off the water.

43. The implication is that this action was repeated again and again. This appears to be a mass-participation form of chunkey rather than the two-man game some later observers describe.

44. *Azumbre* in modern Spanish is a liquid measure of four pints.

45. Fray Andrés's memory failed him in this sentence and in the several that follow it. The governor's name was Domingo Martínez de Avendaño. Asao's head chief was named Domingo in honor of that governor, but his brother, the chief of Talaje, took the name Mateo. See Manuel Serrano y Sanz, *Documentos Históricos de la Florida y la Luisiana, Siglos XVI al XVIII* [Historical documents about Florida and Louisiana, 16th to 18th centuries] (Madrid: Librería General de Victoriano Suarez, 1912), 178.

46. This sentence contains a number of inaccuracies. The Franciscans' work in Florida began in 1573 on a modest scale rather than in 1595. Franciscans established missions at Nombre de Dios and at San Pedro Mocama by 1587, at San Juan del Puerto on Fort George Island shortly thereafter, and worked among the Freshwater Timucua as well. Fray Baltasar López was the friar assigned to San Pedro Mocama. His absence during Andrés de Segura's stay there suggests that he was working elsewhere on Cumberland Island or the adjacent mainland. The friars Andrés mentions as coming from Havana to establish a mission among the Guale had just come from Spain to work in Florida. Andrés's statement is true in the sense that the friars who arrived in 1595 were the first sizeable group in which most of the friars remained in Florida for some years, in contrast to earlier groups, most of whose members escaped from Florida quickly in search of greener pastures.

47. Jesuits had worked among the Guale in the 1560s and the first Franciscans had brief success there in 1573–74, but a prolonged revolt that began in the mid-1570s forestalled further work there until well into the 1680s. Andrés mentions those hostilities obliquely elsewhere in a criticism of the Spanish soldiers' retaliation.

48. This sentence is also partially fallacious and misleading. As was noted above, no mission appears to have been established on the small island where Andrés landed. A mission was established at Asao on the Altamaha River in 1595. And the San Pedro Mocama mission antedates Andrés's visit by eight years.

49. The chief of Asao was not hanged. He was the leader of the Guale who eventually made peace with the Spaniards, though he had killed Asao's friar and led an attack force against San Pedro Mocama with the intention of killing the friar there. The head chief's name was Don Francisco, and the heir was named Juanillo. They were hunted down, killed, and scalped by forces led by chiefs of Asao, Guale, and Tulufina.

50. I have assumed that this *alsó* is the modern *alzó*. It could be rendered in many other ways such as "made off with."

51. *Manto* might be rendered also as *veil*.

52. Albert B. Manucy, trans. (1989), "Narrative of the Hardships Suffered by the People of the *Ship Our Lady of Mercy* in 1595, by Fr. Andrés de San Miguel," in Kathleen A. Deagan, ed., *America's Ancient City: Spanish St. Augustine, 1565–1763*, Spanish Borderland Sourcebooks Ser., no. 25 (New York: Garland Publishing, 1991), 173. In his translation of this passage, Manucy inserts the untranslated Spanish word *cadalecho* at this point, substituting it for the word *catre* or *cot* that Fray Andrés used here.

53. Manucy, ibid., 173, edited García's text here again in rendering (*nros*) as *their,* giving no indication that he was tampering with the text. *Nros* is clearly the abbreviation for *our* or *ours.*

54. This alludes to the Inca Garcilaso de la Vega, the author of *La Florida del Inca.*

55. Manucy, "Narrative of the Hardships," 174, translated this passage very freely as "Before the day was gone, we left."

56. Andrés refers to Fort Caroline built by René Laudonnière in 1564 on the bank of the St. Johns River. See Charles E. Bennett, trans., *Three Voyages: René Laudonnière* (Gainesville: University of Florida Press, 1975), 68–70.

57. This is probably a reference either to the 6 o'clock ringing of the Angelus for the prayer to Mary or the call to Vespers, "The second-last hour of the priest's breviary" or the Evensong of England. Manucy, "Narrative of the Hardships," 174, translated *oración* as *sunset,* again editing García's text.

58. A *chinchorro* is a net made after the fashion of a sweepnet (*barredero*) and similar to a *jabega,* a smaller sweepnet or dragnet.

59. Fray Andrés's soldier informants' account of events involving the French and Spaniards in the 1560s and their relations with Florida's Indians (or the friar's recollection of those details) also departs from the records left by Bartolomé Barrientos, Gonzalo Solís de Merás, and Pedro Menéndez de Avilés himself, all of whom were participants in those events, not to mention the accounts left by their French protagonists. The French were on the scene in the 1560s at Fort Caroline, the forerunner of the Spaniards' San Mateo, prior to the arrival of Menéndez de Avilés. The French had good relations with the Indians in the vicinity of Fort Caroline and northward into southern Georgia. Equally erroneous is Fray Andrés's statement farther on that none of the French based at San Mateo survived.

60. Andrés erred here in identifying the chief actor in these events as "pedro melendez marquez" rather than as "Pedro Meléndez de Avilés." García, in his *Dos Antiguas Relaciones,* 203, placed commas around *marquez,* possibly meaning to suggest thereby that *marquez* there represented the title *marquis* rather than the family name *marquéz.* There is no such punctuation in Fray Andrés's manuscript, which is largely free of punctuation. But it is not certain that that is what García had in mind because he failed to set off *marquéz* with a comma when it reoccurred on p. 204.

61. Whatever Pedro Menéndez's proclivities toward astrology may have been,

he had sounder evidence from friendly Indians. They alerted him to the presence of a group of white men to the south at an estuary they had been unable to cross. See Bartolomé Barrientos, *Pedro Menéndez de Avilés, Founder of Florida*, trans. Anthony Kerrigan (Gainesville: University of Florida Press, 1965), 59. This event occurred later, of course, and was not part of the events leading up to Menéndez's capture of Fort Caroline as Fray Andrés makes it seem here.

62. As the form *polada* does not exist in modern Spanish, in view of the context, I have assumed that it was meant to be *populado*. Fray Andrés had a penchant for truncating the spelling of some words in this fashion.

63. *Sauinas* doubtless was meant to be the modern *sabina*, which refers to trees in the juniper and red cedar families. In this context, however, it seems to refer to cypress.

64. The *canalete* is a single or double-bladed paddle for canoeing.

65. A *sesma* is one-sixth of a Spanish yard or *vara*.

66. The Spanish here is *madera rezia*. *Recia* is the modern form.

67. Fray Andrés's substitution of *toltuga* for the Spanish *tortuga* probably reflects those Indians' languages' lack of the letter *r*.

68. Modern Spanish does not have any pertinent form remotely resembling *Zanbo* or *Zanlo*. Fray Andrés probably was mimicking the Indians' pronunciation of the Spanish word for amber (*ambar*), which is mentioned below as one of the items acquired from the Indians along this coast.

69. *Ligero* might be rendered also as *light* in this context.

70. *Dijeras* was probably meant to be the modern *tijeras* or *scissors*. But another possibility is the modern Spanish word *dije*, which means *trinket*.

71. *Piciete* obviously is related to the modern form *piceo* meaning *pitch*. Congealed pitch or resin is something that resembles amber.

72. The use of the form *sabinos* here reinforces the judgment made in note 63 about the identity of *sauinas*. Again it could refer to cypress, but that rendition is not as strongly indicated here. The most that can be said with certainty is that it involved cedar, juniper, or cypress.

73. The Spanish form *no hierran* used here in *no hierran el aletilla* could be a misspelling of either *hieren*, "they wound," or of *erran*, "they miss." I chose the latter because it makes more sense in this context and because the author spelled *hieren* correctly just two lines above this passage.

74. A finger is about .687 inches or 1/8 of a Spanish yard.

75. Manucy, "Narrative of the Hardships," 185, rendered this passage as "especially for selling to inlanders," interpreting rather than translating.

76. None of the Jesuits in Florida were killed by Indians of south Florida. Indians killed soldiers at Tekesta (Miami) and Tocobaga (Old Tampa Bay). Indians of Virginia killed all but one of the Jesuits who died violently in Menéndez de Avilés's Florida. One of the first three to arrive died at the hands of Mocama just north of the mouth of the St. Johns River. Fray Andrés seems to be confusing this Don Luis with the one who accompanied the Jesuits who went to Virginia; see

John H. Hann, *Missions to the Calusa* (Gainesville: University Press, 1991), 290–92.

77. Rendered literally *gargantas de los pies* again would be *the insteps*.

78. *Ladino* could be rendered also as *crafty* or *cunning*. *Ladino* was a term used often to refer to acculturated Indians or blacks and in such usage could connote *con-man*.

79. A reader has identified him as "Marcos de Aramburu, General of the *Tierra Firme* Fleet. See Chaunu and Chaunu, *Seville et L'Atlantique*, Tome III, 556."

80. García, *Dos Antiguas Relaciones*, 211, interpreted this word as being *baruas*, and, on looking at Fray Andrés's manuscript, I agreed with him initially. As I could not think of any word resembling *baruas* that fits the context, I decided that it might have been meant to be *baruca*, meaning "a trick that one might use to block the effect of something." *Baruca* is derived from *boruca*, meaning shouting or noise. I still consider that as possibly what Fray Andrés had in mind. But I have accepted as possibly more probable John Worth's suggestion that it might be *barcas*. On taking a second look at the manuscript, I decided that a case could possibly be made for interpreting the *u* as *c*.

81. Rangel or Ranjel is a common Spanish or Portuguese name.

82. A reader indicated that this exit from the Bahama Channel occurs opposite Cape Canaveral "at about 28 degrees north latitude."

83. A reader identified the "*arenal* de Sevilla" as "that part of Seville along the river shore by the Torre del Oro." The reader noted that although that area "is built up now, of course, as is the river bank itself, it still bears the name of *Arenal*."

84. *Cabo*, as a term applied to naval officers, formerly had a wide range of possible meanings extending from "commander-in-chief of a division in a squadron" or "the one in charge, no matter what rank he held" to a simple seaman first class who was in charge of a work detail (O'Scanlon, *Diccionario Marítimo Español*, 121).

85. This is the modern Jérez famous for its sherry wine.

86. A reader has observed that Fray Andrés may be referring here "to the Earl of Essex and/or to Lord Charles Howard, both of whom led the 1596 raid on Cádiz."

# Index

*Note: Page numbers in italics indicate map.*

account: dating in, 97n.3, 99n.16; importance of, 16–19; inaccuracies in, 8–9, 99nn.17–18, 101n.48, 101nn.45–46, 49, 102nn.59–60; location of original, 9; overview of, 3–8; translation of, 10. *See also Our Lady of Mercy* (ship); sailors/crew

adviceboat *(patacho)*, 26, 97n.2

Agreda y Sánchez, José María de, 15, 16, 20–22n.19

*Alboroto del Gato* (ship), 84

Altamaha River, 6, *54*

amber, 78, 80, 103n.68

Andrade, José María, 16

Andrade, Vicente de P., 16

Antonio, Prior of Crato (pretender to Portuguese throne), 5, 6, 30

Aranbulo, Marcos de (Marcos de Aramburu), 81, 104n.79

armada: departure from la Habana, 31–32; destruction in Cádiz, 91–94; fate of, 86–88; fleets in, 97–98n.4; leadership for, 89–92; *Our Lady of Mercy* separated from, 33–34. *See also* flagships

Asao, Bar of, *54*

Asao kingdom or province: arrival at, 63–64; assistance from, 6–7, 60, 62–64, 68; departure from, 69–70; move to head chief's village, 66; Spaniards' hostilities, 17, 75

Asao mission, 8, 99n.16, 101n.48

Aztec people, 9

Bahama Channel, 84, 85, 104n.82

Barrientos, Bartolomé, 9, 10, 16, 102n.59

beads, worn by Indians, 64, 80; as trade item, 78

Beristáin y Sousa (Souza), 15–16

black drink or vomiting ceremony, 67–68. *See also cacina*

*cabo* (leader), use of term, 89, 104n.84

*cacina* (drink), 67–68

Cádiz (Spain): destruction of, 8, 89–96; ships' departure from, 25–26, 31, 88–89

Carmelite Order: Andrés's vow to join, 3, 8, 13–14; Andrés's writing preserved by, 15–16

carpenter, 36, 38–39

cat, 17–18, 27–28

catfish, 65

caulker: age of, 41; depression of, 42, 43, 45; repairs by, 59; on weather, 50

Cerralvo, Viceroy Marquis de, 14

*chacal*, use of term, 100n.22. *See also* council houses; *jacal*

chief: frigate visited by one of south Florida, 80; housing of (Guale), 65; naming of (Guale), 101n.45; reception of (Mocama), 70–71

*chinchorro* (sweepnet), 73, 102n.58

chunkey game, 66, 101n.43

clams, Spanish use of, 73

cleric: abandoned, 18, 56; age of, 41, 46; food for, 57; placed in boat, 46; taken to San Pedro, 61

clothing: confiscation of Spaniards', 82–83; description of, for Guale and Mocama, 64, 70, 79, 80; for San Pedro's chief, 70; for south Florida Indians, 79, 80. *See also* Indians, clothing of

Colegio of San Angel, 14, 16
Coloma, Francisco, 31, 82, 88
Condado area (Spain), 98n.12
Convent of the Carmen of Puebla (Car-
melites), 13–14, 15–16
council houses. *See* Indians, council houses
*Crucifix* (ship). *See San Crucifijo de
Burgos* (ship)
Cumberland Island, 7, 99nn.17–18. *See
also* San Pedro Mocama mission
cypress trees, uses of, 76–77

Domingo (chief), 101n.45
*Dos Antiguas Relaciones de la Florida*
(García), 9
Drake, Adm. John, 87–88
drowning, ship captains' indifference to,
3–4

English ships: Cádiz attacked by, 89–96;
confrontations with, 81–83, 87–88; *San
Crucifijo* found by, 29; Spanish captured
by, 7–8, 83–84, 87
*La Escorcelana* (ship), 80–81
Essex, Earl of, 104n.86

Fajardo, Luis, admiral of the Galleons, 30,
84, 88
*felipote* (flyboat), 34
figurine in council house, description of,
67, 75
Filipe (chief), 68
fire in council house, 66
fires, 58–59, 60–62, 66
fish/fishing, 65, 72–73, 78, 79
flagships: changing, 29; choosing, 26–27;
departure of, 31–32; endangered, 29;
sinking of, 29, 86–87
Fleet system, shortcomings of, 3–4, 28–29,
30–31
Florida: coastline of, 85–86; crossing to la
Habana from, 84; prisoners from, 5–6,
29–30, 98n.6
*La Florida del Inca* (Garcilaso de la Vega),
85–86, 102n.54
flyboat *(felipote)*, 34
foremast and bowsprit, loss of, 33

Fort Caroline, 74–75, 102n.56, 102n.59
Fort George Island, 101n.46
Franciscan Order: early missions of, 69,
101nn.46–47; errors on, 8–9; possible
convent site of, 58, 98–99n.15
Francisco (chief), 101n.49
French: attack on, 74–75, 102n.59; forts
of, 71, 73, 102n.56; Indians' relations
with, 73, 102n.59

Galleons, the (*Tierra Firme* Fleet), 31–32,
87, 97–98n.4
García, Genaro: bibliographic work of, 9–
10; translation by, 98nn.7–10, 102n.60,
104n.80
Garcilaso de la Vega (Inca), 85–86,
102n.54
Genaro García Collection, 9
ghost incident, 27–28
God's intervention, 9, 99n.17
gold, 83
González Barcia, Andrés, 15–16
Governor of Florida deposed, 5–6, 29–30
Goropio, Juan, 20–21n.19 (#13)
Guale Indians: description of, 64–65,
100n.29; fires of, 58–59, 60–62, 66;
French and, 73, 102n.59; missions
among, 101nn.46–47; retaliation
against, 17, 75; revolt of, 69, 101n.47,
101n.49; survivors' initial contact with,
6–7, 60. *See also* Asao kingdom or
province
Gulf of Mexico and de Soto, 85

la Habana (Cuba): departure from, 6, 31–
32; as rendezvous spot, 29, 97–98n.4;
return to, 7–8, 77–78, 83–84; wintering
over in, 5, 29–30, 31, 83–84
hairstyle, Indians', 64, 100n.29
horses, 30
House of Trade (Spain), 90
Howard, Lord Charles, 104n.86
hydrography, 3, 9, 14–15

Indians: beds of, 65, 67, 71; body and face
painting by, 64, 67; bows and arrows of,
64–65; cakes of acorn flour, 60, 62;

cakes of maize flour, 60, 62, 66, 68; deerskin, preparation of, 65–66; figurine (Guale), 67, 75; fingernails of, 64; fish weirs of, 72, 73; foot binding by, 64; hair style of, 64, 100n.29; health of, 64; hens among, 64, 65, 66, 68, 100n.29; interpreter, 68; mortars, described, 68; parched corn flour, 68; plaza of, 66; polygyny (Guale), 65; pottery of, 63, 67; red ochre, 64, 67; salt not used by (Guale), 68; skin tone of (Guale), 64; stature of, 64; vomiting ceremony of, 67–68
—clothing of: Guale, 64; Mocamas' chief, 70; men, 65, 79; south Florida Indians, 79–80; women, 64, 65. *See also* clothing
—council houses: of Guale, 63, 65–66, 67; of Mocama, 70–71
—pirogues, 58–59, 60, 61, 62, 70; described, 68; making of, 76–77; paddles for, 77–78, 103n.64; requests for, 63–64, 68
interpreters, 7, 68
Italy, ships from, 89

*jacal,* use of term, 63, 65, 66, 67, 100n.22
Jérez (Xeres de la Frontera), 95, 104n.85
Jesuit Order, 80, 101n.47, 103–4n.76
Juan (chief of Mocama), 70
Juanillo (chief of Guale), 101n.49
Junco, Rodrigo de, 5–6

*ladino,* use of term, 80, 104n.78
Laudonnière, René, 102n.56
launch: attempt to enlarge, 35; commandeering of, 4, 6, 18, 37–40, 53; preparation of, 36–37; survivors in la Habana, 83–84
launch, makeshift: capsizing of, 69–70; construction of, 4, 6, 41–43, 45; landings of, 53–56, 54, 61; launchings of, 45–47, 60; repair of, 58–59; sailing in, 47–51
*lendo,* use of term, 62, 99n.21
Leste, Count de, 95
license for profit, 30, 31
Little St. Simons Island (as possible landing

spot): arrival at, 6, 54, 55–56; finding food on, 56–58, 59; identification of, 98–99n.15; leaving, 58–60
López, Fray Baltasar, 7, 99n.17, 101n.46
Luis (cacique from far south Florida), 80, 103–4n.76
Luis (prince of Portugal), 6

Madariaga, Pedro de, 97n.1
Manucy, Albert B., 102nn.52–53, 55, 103n.75
map of landings, 54
Martín (chiefs' name), 69
Martínez, Enrico, 14, 15
Martínez de Avendaño, Domingo, 6, 7, 69, 101n.45
masts, cutting down, 33–34
Mateo (chief), 69, 101n.45
Medina Sidonia (Spain), 13, 95
Meléndes Marquéz, Pedro, 73–74
Menéndez de Avilés, Pedro: Andres's account compared to, 102n.59; capture of, 102–3n.61; fleet system of, 97–98n.4; identity confused, 9, 102n.60
Menéndez Marqués, Pedro, 6, 9, 102n.60
*Mercy. See Our Lady of Mercy* (ship)
Mesquita, Fray Juan, 7
Mexico: drainage of Valley, 3, 9, 14–15; fleet headed for, 97–98n.4; ship at port in, 5
Mexico City: drainage of, 14–15; report on, 20–21n.19 (#23), 22n.20
Miranda, Gutierre de, 5–6, 29–30, 98n.6
Mocama Indians, 7, 103–4n.76
mullet, 72; method of catching, 79

New France, 86
New Mexico, 86
New Spain: Andrés's second voyage to, 13; coastline of, 85–86; fleet headed for, 25–26, 88–89; shortages in, 26. *See also* Florida
New Spain Fleet, 97–98n.4
New World, allure of, 13
Nombre de Dios mission, 101n.46
*Nra. Señora de la Merced. See Our Lady of Mercy* (ship)

oars, makeshift, 45–46
Ocaa (island), 26
Ospo or Ospogue, 99n.16
*Our Lady of Mercy* (ship): abandonment of, 6, 40, 53; collision of, 32; name of, 4, 52; shipwreck of, 32–35. *See also* launch; launch, makeshift; pumps; sailors/crew
oysters, 57, 58, 59, 62

Padilla, Martín de, 25, 90
La Palma, ship abandoned near, 26, 27, 31
Palma del Condado area (Spain), 98n.12
*patacho* (adviceboat), 26, 97n.2
Philip II (king of Spain), 6
pigs, wild, 57–58
pilot: abandoned, 18, 56; age of, 41, 56; food for, 57; guidance from, 49, 50, 56; injuries of, 44; placed in boat, 46; taken to village, 61; treatment for, 75
pirogues. *See* Indians, pirogues
plaza, chunkey game in, 66, 101n.43
Portugal, flagship from, 89
pottery, 63, 67
prisoners, from Florida, 5–6, 29–30, 98n.6
provisions: cost of, 31; finding of, on island, 56–58, 59; from governor, 71; from Indians, 60–61, 62, 63, 66, 68; for launch, 36–37, 39–40; for makeshift launch, 46, 49–51, 55; rations on makeshift launch, 49–50, 55; at St. Augustine, 7, 72, 76, 77; at San Pedro, 70; for trip from St. Augustine to Havana, 7
Las Puercas (Spain), 89, 90
Puerto Real (Spain), 94
Puerto Rico, attacked by John Drake, 87–88
pumps: design of, 44; limits of, 43; organizing crew to handle, 35, 40–41, 45
purser: character of, 4, 18, 36, 63; crew organized by, 35–36, 40–41, 44, 45, 51, 55; Flemish sailor and, 51–52; God's guidance of, 53; on leaving island, 59; in makeshift launch, 47; requests for pirogue, 63–64, 68

Reynoso Island, 17, 57, 98–99n.15

Rrangel, Francisco, 82, 87, 96
rudder, loss of, 32–33

sailors/crew: commanders' abandonment of, 3–4, 6, 26–27, 40, 86–87; conscription of, 7, 76, 84; discouragement of, 34–35, 41, 42, 43; frigate for, 71–72; Indians' assistance for, 6–7, 60, 62–64, 68; landings of, 53–56, 54; loaded in boat, 46–48; mirage island sighted by, 44–45; organized for tasks, 35–36, 40–41, 44, 45, 51, 55; prayers of, 52–53; problems with, 18, 51–52; remaining on sinking ship, 47–48; return to la Habana, 7–8, 77–78; in St. Augustine, 72–77; at San Pedro, 70–71; splitting up of, 59–69; uncivilized ones of, 35–36. *See also* carpenter; caulker; cleric; pilot; provisions; purser
St. Augustine (Fla.): arrival at, 7, 71–72; crossing to la Habana from, 84; description of, 75–77; location of, 54, 56; mutiny at, 5–6, 29–30, 98n.6; soldiers at, 72–76
St. Elmo's fire, 50
St. Johns River, 71, 102n.56
St. Simons Island, 8, 98–99n.15, 99n.16
Salazar, Capt. Francisco de, 5–6
*San Andrés* (ship), 88
*San Crucifijo de Burgos* (ship): abandonment of, 28–29, 31, 97n.3; description of, 26; identity of, 97n.1
*San Filipe* (ship): burning of, 91, 95; departures of, 31–32, 88; survival of, 87
San Gerónimo, Fray Manuel de, 13, 15
San Juan del Puerto, 101n.46
San Juan de Ulloa (Ulua) (Mexico), 5, 26, 28, 29, 97n.3
*San Martín* (ship): description of, 26–27; launch from, 40; sinking of, 29, 86–87
San Mateo, 54, 71, 73. *See also* Fort Caroline
*San Matias* (ship), 88–89
San Miguel, Fray Andrés: age at shipwreck, 65, 100n.38; character of, 13–14, 17; death of, 15; religious beliefs of, 8–9; vow of, 3, 8, 13–14; work of, 14–

15; writings of, 10, 15–16, 20–22n.19. *See also* account; *Our Lady of Mercy* (ship)
San Pedro Mocama mission: attack on, 101n.49; bench or bed, 71; chief's arrival, 70; council house, 70; dating of, 99n.17; establishment of, 101nn.45, 101n.48; gruel, 70; location of, 54, 99n.18; survivors' journey to, 7, 70–71
Santa Catalina (Spain), 89
Santa Elena, 73
Santa María port (Spain), 89, 95
*Santo Tomás* (ship), 88, 92
Sapelo Island, 98–99n.15
sassafras, 67
seawater, mixed with *cacina*, 67–68
Segura, Andrés de. *See* San Miguel, Fray Andrés
Sestin, Luys, 27
Seville (Spain), 25, 85, 104n.83
sharks, presence of, 37, 48
ships: abandonment of, 6, 25–29, 31, 40, 53, 92–93, 97n.3; collision of, 32; decorations of, 25; fleet system for, 3–4, 97–98n.4; lack of preparation of, 30–31. *See also* English ships; *specific ships*
silver: amount delivered, 88; transportation of, 29, 30, 31–32, 81, 87
soldiers: on events, 73–75; fishing by, 72–73; killed by Indians, 103–4n.76; mutiny in Florida, 5–6, 29–30, 98n.6; number in St. Augustine, 76
Solís de Merás, Gonzalo, 102n.59
Soto, Hernando de, 85–86
south Florida Indians, description of, 79

sweepnet *(chinchorro)*, 73, 102n.58
swordsmith: captured by English, 83–84; ships owned by, 25–26, 32

Talaje, 8
Tekesta (Miami), 103–4n.76
Tenochtitlan, 9
*Tierra Firme* Fleet (the Galleons), 32, 87, 97–98n.4
Timucua Indians, 101n.46. *See also* San Pedro Mocama
Tocobaga (Old Tampa Bay), 103–4n.76
Torquemada, Fray, 69
trading, Indian-Spanish, 77–78, 80–81

University of Texas Latin American Collection Library, 9

villages, burning of, 17, 75. *See also* Asao village

wailing, for chief, 70–71
well linings, 76
whale, hunting of, 79
wine, 26
Wolf Island (as possible landing spot): arrival at, 6, 54, 55–56; finding food on, 56–58, 59, 62; identification of, 98–99n.15; leaving, 58–60
Worth, John E.: on island mission, 99n.16; on landing site, 98–99n.15; on translation, 99n.19, 104n.80

Xega Indians, 79
Xeres de la Frontera (Jérez), 95, 104n.85

John Hann is site historian at Mission San Luis in Tallahassee. He is the author or coauthor of five successful UPF books, including *Missions to the Calusa* (1991) and *A History of the Timucua Indians and Missions* (1996).